The Key to Kenya

– including Tanzania and Zimbabwe

REG & MARY BUTLER

In Association with
THOMSON HOLIDAYS

SETTLE PRESS

Text © 1994 Reg Butler
3rd edition 1997

First published by Settle Press
10 Boyne Terrace Mews
London W11 3LR

ISBN (Paperback) 1 872876 56 0

Printed by Villiers Publications
19 Sylvan Avenue
London N3 2LE

Maps and line drawings by Mary Butler

Foreword

Thomson are happy to be associated with Reg Butler's new book 'The Key to Kenya, Tanzania & Zimbabwe'. In writing the book, the author worked closely with experts who have year-round contact with holiday-makers' travel interests.

Whichever of these beautiful countries you have chosen to visit, we feel this pocket book can act as a quick reference guide to their unique combination of game-viewing and beaches.

When the holiday is over, we suggest you keep the guide-book to help plan your return visit – perhaps at a different season, to see a contrasting range of mammals and birdlife. In one or two weeks, a visitor can explore only a relatively small proportion from the fabulous choice of game reserves in Kenya and the neighbouring areas of Tanzania.

All prices mentioned in the text were accurate at the time of printing. But like so many other areas of the world, Kenya has an inflation problem, and local prices may change during the coming year. However, any costs quoted in the book can serve as guidance to the average level of expenses.

THOMSON HOLIDAYS

Contents

EAST & CENTRAL AFRICA

Chapter One

Introducing Kenya

Kenya is acclaimed as the big success story of African tourism. The country is blessed with great natural attractions: superb climate, beaches, great mountains and lakes, beautiful scenery. But the jackpot is Game Reserves, opening up the chance to watch and photograph wild animals, roaming freely in their natural habitat.

Kenya's 59 National Parks and Reserves occupy 7% of the country's land area. These are vast tracts of wilderness set aside for the preservation of flora and fauna. They provide sanctuary for species as diverse as the bushbaby, the hippo, the tiny carmine bee eater (a ravishing bird) or the dikdik (which looks like Bambi) besides giraffe, cheetah and zebra.

All the 'Big Five' are there – elephant, buffalo, leopard, lion and rhino.

Specially memorable is the enormous range of birdlife. Owing to the great range of habitat – from the humid coastline of the Indian Ocean, to the snow-clad peak of 17,057-ft Mount Kenya – the plains, forests, rivers and lakes are host to well over 1,000 species of bird including winter migrants from Europe. Even the non-expert can soon tick off a list of fifty or more African birds, gorgeous in their colouring. For the dedicated bird-watcher, Kenya is one of the world's greatest venues.

In recent decades, the old-time concept of a Game Reserve – setting aside vast areas as a non-hunting paradise for animals – has undergone a fundamental change. Formerly, many of the Reserves had only minimum facilities for visitors, who were not encouraged.

But as a game warden said: "Today we cannot tie up the land for animals alone, but must justify the land usage as an economic proposition." In modern terms, tourism is Kenya's most valuable cash crop, earning even more than coffee.

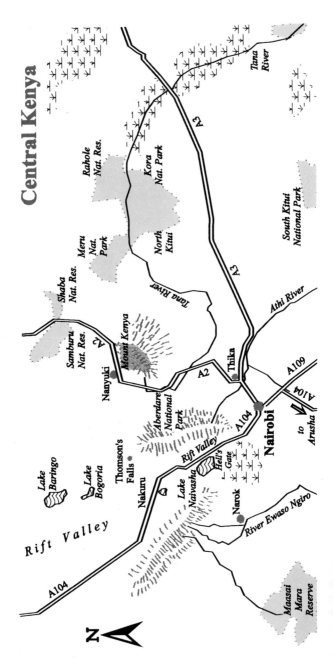

Central Kenya

8

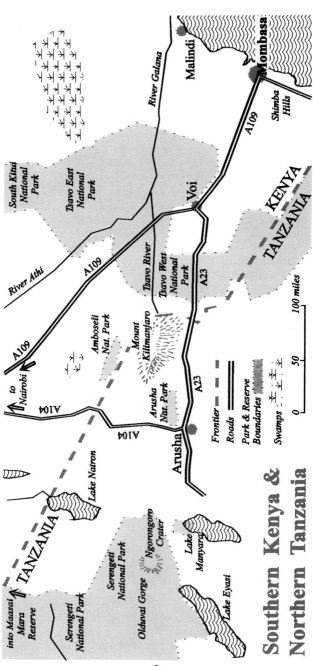

Southern Kenya & Northern Tanzania

Mombasa

Malindi

River Galama

Shimba Hills

A109

Voi

KENYA

TANZANIA

South Kitui National Park

Tsavo East National Park

Tsavo River

Tsavo West National Park

A23

River Athi

A109

Amboseli Nat. Park

Mount Kilimanjaro

A23

to Nairobi

A109

A104

A104

Arusha Nat. Park

Arusha

Lake Natron

TANZANIA

into Maasai Mara Reserve

Serengeti National Park

Serengeti National Park

Olduvai Gorge

Ngorongoro Crater

Lake Manyara

Lake Eyasi

Frontier
Roads
Park & Reserve Boundaries
Swamps

0   50   100 miles

9

INTRODUCTION

Wildlife income

With relatively small capital expenditure on overnight accommodations, dirt roads and easily-constructed viewing platforms near waterholes, the yield in foreign currencies is considerable. The African tribesman can clearly see that tourists on safari bring money into a region, spending on accommodation, food, services, transport and handicraft souvenirs.

Hence the government and people of Kenya are well aware of that basic equation: wild animals bring in tourists; no animals, no tourists. Hence the unpopularity of the poacher, who is no longer a local hero!

Regrettably, the rhino and elephant populations suffered badly when the sale of tusks, hunting trophies and the hides of many beautiful animals was an accepted part of international trade. Since then, countries with a respect for wildlife conservation have banned that commerce, though an international black market still continues for rhino and elephant tusks.

Meanwhile the Kenyan government in more recent times has shown a firm commitment to a policy of "conserving the natural environments of Kenya and their fauna and flora, for the benefit of present and future generations and as a world heritage".

In 1989 the eminent anthropologist, Dr. Richard Leakey, was appointed Director of Kenya's Wildlife Conservation and Management Department. The achievements of Dr Leakey and his Kenya Wildlife Service (KWS) have been considerable. Poaching in Kenya has been almost entirely eliminated and the threatened elephant and black rhino populations are now recovering. Visiting animal lovers themselves have played an active part by contributing to a "Save the Rhino Fund" which helped meet the cost of Kenya's Rhino Rescue Project.

Friends of Conservation

Supporting the work of preserving the wildlife and the environment is the international charity called Friends of Conservation.

FOC has been specially active in backing campaigns to eliminate rhino poaching. On the educational front, FOC funds a programme in local schools to teach the next generation the value of preserving the environment for the sake of the future. An ongoing project aims to stop tourist vehicles from harassing wildlife. Even the largest animals come under stress when surrounded or pursued by safari buses.

Thomson is backing the FOC's work by donating £5 for every passenger who takes a Kenyan holiday. It helps ensure the survival of wildlife which has roamed the plains for thousands of years, and which is now under such pressure from mankind. For more details about Friends of Conservation, phone 0171 730 7904.

Heritage

A tourist official said: "Africa's wildlife is just as much the heritage of mankind as the great masterpieces of painting in the art galleries of Europe.

"Just as no country would auction off its National Gallery for the sake of easy hard currency, so the idea of invading the Reserves for easy meat is 'out'."

In the late 20th century, it has become as simple to travel through Africa, taking pictures of elephants, zebras, wildebeest and giraffes, as to go through Europe taking colour-slides and movies of cathedrals and castles.

Game safaris

In former times, revenue came mainly from a small number of wealthy travellers on very expensive hunting safaris. Today's game-viewing safaris yield considerably more income to Africa than the old-time hunters, even with their very high licence fees.

On a game-viewing drive, there is potential excitement round every bend of the trail: a great herd of wildebeest, perhaps; or a dozen zebra, grazing within thirty yards of the track; or a pause while giraffes lope across the route.

Great pleasure comes from the wealth of nature lore poured forth by a good safari driver-guide. He can be equally interesting about the spoor of a lion or the serpentine track of an elephant's trunk that has trailed in the dust, as about the habits of the dung-beetle.

Park accommodation

There is wide variety in the style of accommodation in game parks. In the principal game reserves, visitors can stay at comfortable lodges, small hotels or tented camps. Other parks feature groups of well-built thatched huts, furnished with twin beds, wash-basin, table and chairs.

Chapter Two

Planning to go

2.1 Which season?

Kenya, covering an area 2½-times the size of Britain, is a year-round destination. Within that vast territory, ranging from the narrow belt of coastal lowlands to the snow-clad slopes of 17,057-ft Mount Kenya, there is great variation in landscape and climate.

In the north and east, bordering Ethiopia and Somalia, parched deserts receive less than 10 inches of rain a year. In contrast, some parts of the Kenya Highlands collect up to 60 inches, depending on elevation and exposure to moisture-bearing winds.

The Mombasa coast averages some 50 inches annually, compared with much of the plains at around 20 inches. Conditions can vary from sweltering humidity on the coast, to cold mornings in the central highlands and bone-dry heat in the northern deserts.

It's that wide climatic diversity which explains the great range of animal life in the varied habitats of lakes, rivers, plains, forest, swamp, desert and coast.

There are two rainy seasons: the long rains between April and June, when seaweed builds up on the beaches due to monsoon winds; and the short rains in November and early December, mainly in the highlands.

Mombasa has a very comfortable climate from June through to September. It's then not too hot and humid, although there may be some afternoon rain – typically tropical, in buckets but of short duration. It's nature's way of air conditioning, refreshing and welcome: clearing the air, and perking up the flowers.

After a daytime downpour, the sun rapidly reappears and everything soon dries out. Sunshine averages eight hours a day, year round. The hottest, driest months are January and February.

What weather to expect – Highlands and Coast

Max — Average maximum daytime temperatures— °F.
Min — Average minimum night-time temperatures— °F.
Sun — Average daily hours of sunshine.

Rain — Average monthly rainfall in inches.
Days — How many days a month with rain.
Humid — Average monthly percentage humidity.

Nairobi	Jan	Feb	Mar	Apr	May	Jun	Jul	Aug	Sep	Oct	Nov	Dec	Annual rainfall
Max	75	79	79	75	73	72	70	72	75	77	73	73	
Min	52	52	55	57	55	52	48	50	50	54	55	54	
Sun	9	9	8	7	6	6	4	4	6	7	7	8	
Rain	1.5	2.5	4.9	8.3	6.2	1.8	0.6	0.9	1.2	2.1	4.3	3.4	37.8"
Days	5	6	11	16	17	9	6	7	6	8	15	11	
Humid	44	40	45	56	62	60	58	56	45	43	52	53	

Mombasa	Jan	Feb	Mar	Apr	May	Jun	Jul	Aug	Sep	Oct	Nov	Dec	Annual rainfall
Max	90	90	91	88	84	84	82	82	84	86	88	90	
Min	73	73	75	75	73	73	72	72	72	72	73	73	
Sun	9	9	9	8	6	8	7	8	9	9	9	9	
Rain	1.0	0.7	2.5	7.7	12.6	4.7	3.5	2.6	2.5	3.4	3.8	2.4	47.4"
Days	6	3	7	15	20	15	14	16	14	10	10	9	
Humid	66	63	63	71	76	72	72	72	70	69	69	69	

PLANNING TO GO

Winter warmth

Despite being so close to the equator, Nairobi is relatively cool because of the 5,450-ft altitude.

Both for the coastal resorts and the game reserves, there's a peak season around Christmas, when many visitors follow the birds to escape the European winter. Low season for the coast goes from April till mid-June, and November till mid-December – covering the two main periods of heavier rains. The same pattern applies to safari holidays, where rain reduces the chances of seeing wildlife amid the rich cover of greenery.

Incidentally, owing to Kenya's proximity to the equator, days and nights are of similar length. Plus or minus ten minutes, sunrise comes at 6.30 a.m., sunset at 6.30 p.m. Year-round it's dark by 7 p.m.

2.2 Arrival in Kenya

Direct flights from Heathrow are operated by British Airways' Boeing 747 or Kenya Airways' Airbus; and from Gatwick and Manchester by Britannia Airways' Boeing 767. Flight time from the United Kingdom is around 9 hours to Mombasa or Nairobi.

Entry Requirements

A valid passport and a return or onward ticket is required by all persons entering Kenya. Passports should be valid for six months after your arrival date. A visa is not required by British citizens.

Commonwealth citizens are likewise exempt from visas, except those from Australia, New Zealand, Canada, Nigeria or Sri Lanka. Visas are required for some European and other nationalities. Visitors must be inoculated against Yellow Fever if they come from an infected area such as Tanzania, and cholera and typhoid certificates are recommended but not essential.

For guests flying to Nairobi on a scheduled flight, walk through the terminal building following signs for arrivals and immigration. If you have not been given a landing card on the plane, collect and complete one at the immigration barrier. Immigration will give you a stamp normally valid for the length of your holiday.

Passengers arriving by charter aircraft will usually fly direct to Mombasa, and will go through a similar immigration check before changing to a domestic Air Kenya scheduled service to Nairobi.

Customs control

Continue into the baggage hall, where luggage trolleys are available. Collect your bags and pass through Customs. The officers rarely go through tourists' luggage, but it may happen. Returning Kenyan residents are searched thoroughly, so try not to get behind them in the Customs queue. Otherwise, expect a long wait!

Allowances are standardised at 200 cigarettes or other tobacco equivalent; and one litre of alcohol.

Passengers with a video camera must fill in a declaration form on arrival. If they no longer possess the camera on departure, they will be required to pay the equivalent value of the camera. Other electrical appliances may be entered on passports and items must be produced to Customs before departing. A refundable deposit or a Customs bond may be required.

Meeting the reps

At the exit from Customs, you are met by tour escorts for transfer to your hotel. Should the representative not be immediately visible, wait near the doors. Thomson's local agents are United Touring Company, a very large company which has been operating in Kenya for years. The reps will usually be wearing Thomson uniforms. But occasionally they may be wearing the green uniform of UTC, and holding a Thomson clipboard.

If you are flying onwards from Nairobi to Mombasa, customs and immigration are cleared in Nairobi. It's just a short walk to the domestic terminal. On the return journey the check-in is sometimes carried out in Mombasa but usually in Nairobi.

Independent travellers will always find taxis awaiting at the airport. Before accepting any offers of transport, ask the Information Desk for guidance on what standard price to pay. Avoid being scalped!

For those clients immediately going on safari upon arrival, it is advisable to bring two small pieces of luggage with you, rather than one large item. You can then leave one bag to be transported to your beach hotel. However, it will only be accepted if it is locked.

Departure formalities

Looking ahead to final departure, a Departure Tax is levied of US$20, or the equivalent in other hard currency. Thomson Holidays includes these charges in the cost of the holiday package, and pay them on their clients' behalf. Other travellers should be prepared for this tax requirement.

If you are not accompanied to the airport by your tour rep, the agency will be there at the airport to assist, and will pay the airport departure tax. Make sure the tax stamp has been attached to your ticket.

Check-in can be a slow business, as all luggage must be identified and inspected before you can go through Passport Control. Complete a departure card for Immigration, and hand it in.

Seat numbers will not be allocated until after you have passed through Security. There are limited bars and cafes in all terminal buildings both land and air-side, and a small duty free shop.

2.3 Changing money

Currency is the Kenya Shilling, which divides into a hundred cents, like splitting the atom. The exchange rate at the time of printing was about 90 Kenyan Shillings to the pound sterling, or 55 to the US dollar. So don't bother about counting Kenyan cents.

The largest banknote is for 1,000 Shillings, then notes for 500, 200, 100, 50, 20 and 10. Kenyan coins are 5 Shillings, 1 Shilling, 50 cents, 10 and 5 cents.

Although there are banks in both Nairobi and Mombasa airports, the queues can be very long. If so, wait until you reach your hotel before changing into Shillings. Beware, however, of the commission that many hotels charge for currency exchange. If possible go to a bank instead. They are open 9-14 hrs Mon-Fri, and also 9-11 hrs on the first and last Saturday of the month. Do not exchange money with street dealers – they are usually con-men.

Well-known credit cards such as Visa, MasterCard, American Express and Diners are accepted at most hotels, restaurants, lodges and some shops.

On safari it's quite common for the lodges to run out of money! So it's advisable to change some money in Nairobi or Mombasa before you set off, although you shouldn't need large amounts of cash.

Any remaining Kenyan Shillings can be exchanged back into sterling or other currency only at the airport banks, on production of exchange receipts issued by official changers. To avoid queues, try to wind down your local funds as the time of departure approaches.

2.4 What to wear and pack

The Kenyan coast can be hot and humid, so beach and casual clothing is the order of the day. Bring both bits of bikini, as topless is illegal. Ultra-brief shorts and beachwear should not be worn in town. Pack cover-ups for shopping trips, excursions or snacks at the bar.

Evenings tend to be smarter, but still casual. Jackets are not required at coast hotels, but long trousers are recommended as evening defence against mosquitoes. Light-weight suits and dresses, and casual loose fitting cotton clothes are ideal. But take a sweater for the chill of air-conditioned restaurants.

Most hotels provide towels for use by the pool, or there may be a small charge. But consider packing beach towels for sampling other beaches. Plastic shoes are useful for walking on the beach and paddling at low tide. They are invaluable for underwater sports, as the corals are quite sharp. However, these shoes are readily available and inexpensive to buy locally.

If you intend to do any exploring on foot, bring a comfortable and sturdy pair of shoes or trainers.

The majority of sports equipment can be hired once in resort. If you are particularly keen on specific sports, pack any personal equipment you may need: tennis or snorkelling gear, for instance.

Unexpected downpours of rain can be very refreshing, and quite enjoyable if you are ready equipped with a plastic mac or an umbrella. Even more useful is a hat to keep the sun at bay, though souvenir headgear can easily be bought on arrival.

On safari, shoes should be low-heeled, comfortable and closed-toed. Socks, slacks, sun-hats, sunglasses and sun-oil are also recommended. A hat that you can tie on won't fly off when you're driving around in an open-top safari vehicle.

A cotton tracksuit is useful for early-morning game drives which sometimes start before dawn. Gentlemen are required to wear long trousers for dinner in the safari lodges. At the higher altitudes, temperatures drop substantially after sundown – much cooler than on the coast – so a warm sweater is well worth packing.

Laundry service is readily available in all the hotels, and most of the lodges. Simply leave a message for the maid and allow 24 hours for laundering. Charges are about £1 for a shirt and £1.50 for trousers or skirt.

Other items to pack

Don't forget suntan lotion and any medicines which you take regularly. Supplies in the safari lodges are very limited, so ensure you have sufficient to last for the entire holiday. Even if your favourite brands are available in Nairobi or Mombasa, they are very likely to be more expensive than back home.

A more complete kit could include moisturising creams, travel sickness pills and some stomach upset tablets such as Imodium or Lomotil; chapstick, insect repellent, sting relief; plasters and antiseptic cream.

A final reminder: bring a supply of reading matter, plenty of film, and ensure you have fresh batteries in your camera. Photo supplies and books cost more in Kenya. On safari, binoculars are invaluable for game and bird viewing, though each mini bus carries one pair.

2.5 Health care

There is no *obligation* to produce vaccination certificates when arriving in Kenya direct from Europe or North America. But jabs for hepatitis are recommended, and vaccination records should be checked on whether you still have protection against typhoid, polio and tetanus. In addition, clients for Tanzania and Zanzibar must produce a valid Yellow Fever certificate. At the time of going to press, the Foreign Office also recommends inoculations against rabies.

Ask your own doctor's advice at least six weeks before departure. Some medical people lean heavily towards ultra-caution, and recommend the full works. Others suggest that some of these precautions are not essential if you are taking normal care of yourself, and not visiting any outlandish areas.

For further health advice contact the Hospital for Tropical Diseases Healthline on 0839 337 722. Code number is 55. The phone charge is 49p a minute.

Malaria

Precautions are essential, to cover the risk in coastal areas. Nairobi and the Highlands are comparatively safe. A course of anti-malaria pills should be started a week before departure, and be religiously taken to the timetable specified by the doctor, during and after a trip to Kenya.

Mosquitoes

Quite apart from the dreaded female *anopheles* mosquitoes who are responsible for spreading malaria, it's worth having your defences ready against all the other varieties of biting insects. Mosquitoes and sand flies bite especially at dusk when hungry for supper. They are very partial to holidaymakers. It's wise to be frugal in use of perfumes and aftershaves, as these seem to attract them. Insect repellents are sold at chemists and in hotel-resort shops.

An excellent mosquito deterrent is (believe-it-or-not) Avon's 'Skin-so-soft' bath oil spray. It's highly effective. Even sand-flies will keep their distance.

For a peaceful night's sleep, keep your windows closed after dark, and have any mosquito screens in place. In accommodation which relies upon mosquito nets around your bed, ensure that the net is properly tucked in.

Leave the air conditioner switched on. It's worth packing an electrically-operated mosquito kit, which can be remarkably effective, vapourising an insect repellent throughout the night. The kits are usually available in the airport shops when you depart from UK. Don't encourage other insects by leaving food around in your room.

Sun and health

Deep suntan is often regarded as a sign of health, but doctors advise caution against overdoing it, because of skin-cancer risk. To avoid sunburn, the standard advice is well enough known. But many holidaymakers don't fully realise the power of the equatorial sun, which can still burn even if you are sitting in the shade, where bright sunshine can be reflected off water or sand. Ultraviolet rays can also strike through clouds, though a heavy overcast sky offers some protection.

When working on your sun tan, go easy for the first few days. Take the sun in very small doses and wear a wide-brimmed sun hat, or a baseball-type cap. Take extra care whenever your shadow is shorter than your height. The shorter your shadow, the more risk of sunburn. Avoid the UV danger time between noon and 2 p.m. Resume your sunbathing late afternoon when the sun is not so strong.

Use plenty of high-factor suntan lotion – SPF of 15 or over – reapplied every hour or so after you've been in the pool. Wear a T-shirt while swimming or using a snorkel. If your exposed skin has turned pink or red by evening, be more careful next day!

Hopefully you'll go home with a tan that's golden and not lobster red or peeling.

In case of heatstroke – marked by headache, flushed skin and high temperature – get medical advice. Meanwhile wrap yourself in wet towels, and drink fruit juice or water.

Finally, beware of iced drinks while sunbathing, and then jumping in the pool. Your tummy is bound to rebel.

Water

Tap water is pure enough if your stomach is accustomed to any Kenyan ingredients. The water is chlorinated, and may cause some stomachs to protest until accustomed to the flavour. Otherwise it's best to be cautious. Hotels and lodges can provide reliable cold water in flasks at your bedside. And there's usually nothing to worry about in the drinks and ice cubes served in hotels and good restaurants. Bottled mineral water is also available, but very expensive – could be £2 a bottle in hotels, and £1-£2 in supermarkets.

Stomach upsets

Most upsets are caused by unaccustomed food, very cold drinks and hot sun. If you're not accustomed to quantities of fresh fruit, go easy at first with all that tempting tropical produce. Give your stomach time to attune itself to a deluge of pineapple juice and fruit punches. That also applies if you are not used to Kenya coffee. Take it in small amounts for the first few days. Be wary about down-market local restaurants, where kitchen standards may be less than ideal.

If you want to come prepared, bring pharmaceuticals such as Lomotil, Imodium or Arrêt, which are usually effective. Imodium can be bought at any UK chemists.

Usually the problem takes 24 hours to clear up. If your stomach is still complaining after a couple of days, see a doctor. There's no point in suffering. He'll fix you with tablets or an injection.

Local problems

The HIV virus that causes Aids is extremely prevalent in both sexes. Yielding to unprotected temptation is like playing Russian roulette.

Chapter Three

Nairobi

3.1 'City in the Sun'

Nairobi, capital of Kenya, is 310 miles from the Indian Ocean and 87 miles south of the Equator. With well over a million population – possibly two million – it is the largest city between Cairo and Johannesburg.

The 'City in the Sun' enjoys an almost perfect tropical climate, with the heat modified by 5,500-ft altitude. Day temperatures are never uncomfortably high, and humidity is low. The nights are cool and refreshing.

Nairobi is a Maasai word meaning 'The Place of Cool Waters'. The vibrant city centre is overlooked by hotels of international standard, skyscraper office blocks and imposing civic buildings.

Parks, gardens and main boulevards are planted with oleanders, hibiscus and other shrubs. There are hedges everywhere of bougainvillaea – orange, red, cerise, white and pink.

Less than a century ago, the area was just an open swamp which a Royal Engineer sergeant chose as a depot for the building of the Mombasa-Uganda railway. The railhead reached Nairobi in 1899, and camp followers, traders, adventurers and settlers made the construction camp and depot their headquarters. Eight years later it became the capital of Kenya, taking over from Mombasa.

Nairobi is the holiday and safari base for most visitors to East Africa. From the capital you can plan your itinerary, buy all you need and make any travel booking anywhere. Most visitors stay just a day or two, before departing on a wildlife safari or for a period of relaxation on the coast.

Shops are generally open from 8.15 to 17.30 hrs, and most close for lunch from 13-14 hrs. Some stay open Saturday afternoons and Sunday mornings, particularly the souvenir and curio shops and the Municipal Markets. Central areas are well supplied with eager street vendors.

3.2 Sightseeing

Most of Nairobi's sightseeing can be covered in a day. The essential sightseeing includes the city centre, laid out in grid pattern and marked by the broad avenues of Kenyatta, Moi and Haile Selassie. The main shopping areas can be explored, while making time for visits to your choice of the National Museum, the nearby Snake Park and Aviary, and the Railway Museum.

Other places of interest are the City Hall, Parliament Buildings, Law Courts, McMillan Memorial Library, University of Nairobi, Anglican and Roman Catholic cathedrals, and the beautiful white and silver Jamia Mosque.

Behind the Mosque lies the spice-scented Bazaar and nearby is the Municipal Market with its stalls of fruit, vegetables, hand-woven baskets and wood carvings. There are beautiful displays of cut flowers of all kinds and colours: roses, marigolds, carnations, gladioli, arum lilies.

A guided city sightseeing tour, or a few hours at the Nairobi National Park will help you get the feel of the country before setting off on your safari.

For visitors who stay longer, facilities are excellent for all kinds of sport, including horse and motor racing, dinghy sailing and golf.

Evening entertainment includes discos and night clubs, gaming and cabaret at the International Casino, and a wide range of good restaurants.

The Kenyatta International Conference Centre is the city's skyscraper focal point. It covers a large area, including government buildings and gardens. If possible, go to the 27th or 28th floor for a bird's-eye view of the city.

The Railway Museum houses East Africa's first steam locomotive, and the actual first-class carriage from which a railway superintendent was dragged by a man-eating lion.

The National Museum has fine exhibits of East African fauna, birds, fish, prehistoric remains and minerals. If you are interested in the discoveries of early man, made by the Leakey family, the full story is displayed here, together with Tanzanian rock paintings.

There is also a good collection of tribal ornaments, weapons, and headdresses, including the Maasai warrior's traditional lion-mane creation.

Upstairs, too, are Joy Adamson's original paintings of Kenya's ethnic peoples, as well as her botanical paintings.

The Snake Park displays live snakes from Africa and Asia in glass cages or pits, besides tortoises, crocodiles and other reptiles. Some humdrum fish tanks could be described as an Aquarium.

The Arboretum, just outside the city centre, has a wide range of indigenous and exotic trees, while the Central and City Parks display many of the flowers, shrubs and succulent plants of East Africa.

3.3 Nairobi National Park

Believe it or not, many Nairobi residents live further from the City Centre than the wildlife in Nairobi National Park. Only eight miles from the towering office blocks and hotels of downtown Nairobi, this unique Park covers 44 square miles of sweeping grassy plains, acacia bush, steep gorges and wooded streams. It is bounded southwards by the Athi River, and by forest in the north. There is unrestricted movement of game in and out of the area to the south.

Herds of zebra, wildebeest, impala and gazelle, with giraffe, warthog and eland range through the Park. The quiet dark forest abounds with bushbuck, waterbuck and sometimes leopard. Baboon and vervet monkeys are found throughout the Park, and rock hyrax in the gorges. The Athi River has many hippo and crocodile. Park Rangers will direct you to the main camera targets, lion and cheetah.

The Park's birdlife is varied and beautiful with ostrich, sunbirds and many species of water birds near the pools and dams. An Animal Orphanage stands at the main gate of the Park, where semi-tame, sick, orphaned or abandoned animals are cared for.

Chapter Four

Game parks galore

4.1 The safari experience

'Safari' is a good Swahili word for an overland journey or expedition. In prewar days that mainly meant the rich man's sport of shooting big game. But today a huge choice of safaris is available to middle-income travellers, shooting with cameras.

If you are thrilled by wild-animal films on cinema and TV screens, it's now easier than ever before to sample the African adventure first-hand.

The standard safari minibus is custom built and is equipped with game viewing hatches, sliding windows, binoculars and a first aid kit.

The driver is also your guide, speaking English, knowing the routes, where to spot animals and how to recognise them. He will ensure that you see as much game as is possible during your travels with him. If you want any advice or assistance whilst on safari, do not hesitate to ask.

Most drivers have over 10 years' experience. Their training is continually updated in the fields of game tracking, photography, first aid and vehicle maintenance.

Rough rides

The roads on safari are rough, bumpy and dusty – partly in order to restrict speedy driving and partly to preserve the natural state of the parks. Game drives usually start early since early morning and late afternoon are the best times for viewing wildlife. The animals sleep during the hottest part of the day.

You may not always see every animal you expect – especially if the weather changes or a particular species is migrating. In some areas you are allowed to leave the safari vehicle. But generally you cannot, although the open roof will enable you to see the game clearly and take photographs.

Clothing

Take warm clothing on safari, including a sweater or two and a light jacket, for morning and evening game drives. Midday can get hot, so wear layers you can peel off. A hat and scarf are useful for protection against dust and sun.

Other useful items are a torch, an alarm clock and socks and long trousers for evening protection against insect bites. Take a couple of cans of good insect repellent (Autan, for instance) for daily use, particularly in the evening and during the rainy season.

Luggage

We advise Safari passengers to travel to Kenya with two smaller cases rather than one large one. Clothes for the beach can be left at your hotel in Nairobi or with your rep at Mombasa airport, who will ensure that spare cases are waiting at your hotel after the safari. Laundering is normally fast and inexpensive.

Your Safari Lodge

All the lodges have quite a high degree of comfort – more than you may expect. Most have bar facilities and a laundry service. In the evenings there is little laid-on entertainment, but talk of the day's sightseeing, amid such original surroundings, is enough to amuse most people! Some lodges overlook watering holes which are floodlit at night. Guests are asked to remain quiet so as not to scare away the animals which may come to watering holes close by.

Tented camps are also quite luxurious and a far cry from a Boy Scouts camp. They have the added advantage of giving a truly African experience, whilst still enabling you to dip in the pool or sip a cool drink.

A typical tent measures 15´ by 10´, zipped front and back, with a floor. The loo, wash-basin and shower is in brick surround at rear. The walls are not roofed, so that you shower in semi open-air. Dinner is by candlelight. A highlight of the stay is after dinner drinks around the campfire, listening to the sound of the African night. A hurricane lamp hangs outside each tent, and a watchman keeps the fire going till dawn.

4.2 Tsavo National Park

With an area of 8,000 sq miles – larger than Wales – Tsavo National Park is the largest in Kenya, and one of the world's greatest wildlife sanctuaries. Located

GAME PARKS

midway between Nairobi and Mombasa, open plains alternate with savannah bush and semi desert scrub, with areas of lush riverine and swamp vegetation.

Established in 1948, the Park is split by the Mombasa-Nairobi road into Tsavo East (north of the highway) and Tsavo West (south of the road). **The River Tsavo** flows through Tsavo West; **River Galana** in Tsavo East. Numerous smaller streams drain from Mount Kilimanjaro, just across the border in Tanzania.

Until a major onslaught by poachers during the 1980's, Tsavo could claim the world's largest concentration of elephants, between 15,000 and 20,000. Numbers have been reduced to under 4,000, with massive slaughter especially of mature adults. Hopefully the tighter control of poaching will now enable the herds to re-establish themselves.

Numerous other species flourish in the Park, to ensure extremely interesting game-viewing drives.

Wildlife includes Lesser Kudu, Buffalo, Common Waterbuck, Eland, Impala, Klipspringer, Oryx, Zebra, Maasai Giraffe, Gerenuk, Hippopotamus, Lion.

Birdlife includes Taita Falcon, Weaver, Barbet, Pygmy Geese, Black Heron.

Tsavo West

The main entrance to Tsavo West is at Mtito Andei. A direct road leads to Kilaguni Lodge and Kitani Lodge, where Mzima Springs attract a good variety of wildlife besides providing much of the water supply of Mombasa, over 100 miles away.

Groups of hippo bask in the crystal clear pools, and shoals of barbel and other fish can be watched through the glass of an observation tank at the water's edge, where visitors can get a duck's-eye view of the reeds. There are lizards in the area, and yellow baboons.

Close by is Poacher's Lookout, a hilltop location with a telescope for spotting game, and a splendid panoramic view looking towards snow-capped Kilimanjaro.

Kilaguni Lodge faces the volcanic Chyulu Hills. Guests are greeted on their verandahs by superb glossy starlings and red-beaked hornbills, hoping for food. Swallows nest under the roof, and baboons come visiting. There are lizards, bats and rock hyrax.

The floodlit waterhole and saltlick are patronised by zebra, wart hogs, oryx, maribou storks, lion, cheetah and hyena.

Ngulia Lodge is set 1,600 feet above the plains, on the edge of the Ndawa Escarpment. It offers spectacular viewing over the surrounding countryside. A variety of animals drink at the waterhole, including elephant, waterbuck and zebra. On most nights a leopard feeds from a baited tree just outside the lodge; later, a hyena comes for the leftovers.

In Tsavo East, Voi Lodge is superbly situated, overlooking the plains. You can view game on the plain whilst relaxing by the pool.

4.3 Taita Hills

Road access to Taita Hills is via the town of Voi on the main Nairobi-Mombasa highway.   After the turn-off, the countryside becomes more interesting, with huge plantations of sisal which is processed in Voi.

This area was the scene during the first World War of fierce fighting between the Germans and an allied force commanded by General Jan Smuts. The German target was to destroy the railway bridge over the Tsavo River, and thus cut communications between Mombasa and Nairobi. Owing to poor quality maps, the German force never found the bridge, and were finally pushed back to what was then German East Africa, now Tanzania.

Taita Hills game sanctuary is a private estate operated by the Hilton group, with a luxury-grade Taita Hills Lodge at the park entrance. There is massed bougainvillaea in the forecourt, swimming pool, 9 hole golf course and a landing strip for aircraft.

A couple of miles further along, Salt Lick Lodge rates as Kenya's most unusual architectural design for gamepark accommodation. The bedrooms are rondavels on stilts, reached by several bridges and spiral staircases. The lounge has a huge fireplace with log fire and a tall, tall chimney built with stone.

The Lodge is beautifully set overlooking a waterhole frequented by a variety of game, including the popular Grant's gazelle, oryx and zebra. Swifts and martins fly in big groups. After dark comes the constant noise of frogs.

If your next destination is Mombasa, the climatic change is very noticeable: steadily hotter as you drop from an area of 7,000-ft peaks to the coast. Children sell cashew nuts and melons by the roadside.

4.4 Amboseli

A four-hour drive from Nairobi, Amboseli National Park lies in Maasailand, and borders on Tanzania at the base of 19,340-ft Mt Kilmanjaro. One of Kenya's most popular parks, Amboseli is named after the lake which can be driven across in the dry season.

From Nairobi the main highway A 104 via Kajiado travels through flat dry grassland, then scrub. Drivers often halt at Namanga, where some Maasai people will pose for photos. The long, dusty road C 103 passes Lake Amboseli, with chance of seeing a mirage.

Wildlife includes Buffalo, large herds of Elephant, Lion, Maasai Giraffe, Fringe-eared Oryx, Black-faced Vervet Monkey, Yellow Baboon, Gerenuk, Black-backed Jackals, Spotted Hyena, Bat-eared Fox and occasional African hunting dog.

Birdlife includes Over 400 species with water birds and migrants, two rare Vultures, the Taita Falcon and the Southern Banded Harrier Eagle, Madagascar Squacco Heron, Long-toed Lapwing, Bustard, Sandgrouse.

Game-viewing drives are set against the magnificent backdrop of Kilimanjaro – a Chagga name that means 'great white shining mountain'. It comprises three separate volcanoes of different ages. Kibo is the youngest and highest, with a permanent ice cap. Shira, 13,140 ft high, is the oldest. Mawenzi, 16,890 ft, is the toughest to climb. Mountaineers usually approach from the south, at Marangu in Tanzania. Much of the Amboseli area is smothered in volcanic ash, rocks and lava.

4.5 Shimba Hills

This relatively small reserve, area 74 sq miles, is handily placed for easy access from coastal resorts. It's only 25 miles south of Mombasa, in the refreshing hills 1650 ft above Diani Beach.

It was specially established in 1968 to protect the herds of Sable antelope, which are now found nowhere else in Kenya. Other game includes buffalo, leopard and waterbuck, while the forested areas are rich in birdlife. You can feed bush babies when they come to the lodge after dark. From vantage points amid rolling grassland there are splendid views down to the coast. The reserve is very rich botanically with two of Kenya's most beautiful terrestrial orchids.

Shimba Hills Lodge is set in thick forest overlooking a waterhole where elephant and other animals come to bathe and drink. It is built on three floors in dark wood around the existing trees. Although possessing communal bathrooms, the rooms offer an excellent view and the food is very good. In Treetops style there's an elevated walk at tree-branch height to an alternative observation point. From the bar you can feed the bush babies after dark.

Birdlife includes Spring Migration of Cuckoo, Honey Buzzard, Red-backed Shrike.

Wildlife includes Roan Antelope, Buffalo, Bushbaby, Bushbuck, Suni, Sykes Monkey, Duiker, Serval.

4.6 The Aberdares, and Treetops

The Aberdare Mountains thrust out directly north of Nairobi and form most of Aberdare National Park, a wonderland of strange alpine plants and plentiful wildlife which sometimes reaches above 11,000 ft altitude. The Aberdares are part of Kenya's Central Highlands with heavily forested slopes, high waterfalls and moorlands.

En route from Nairobi, a good road passes crops of sunflowers, maize and coffee, growing in the rich rusty-red soil. A stop can be made to view the Chania waterfalls. Into more hill country, there are fields of bananas, pineapples, maize, cabbages and lettuce; and herds of cattle, sheep and goats. All this region is Kikuyu territory.

Outspan Hotel at Nyeri is the base for visiting Treetops. There is beautiful purple bougainvillaea at the drive entrance, and it's worth strolling down towards the Chania River and a waterfall, along a path that passes through an ancient banyan tree. Lord Baden-Powell, founder of the Scout movement, lived in his later years at Paxtu Cottage in the hotel grounds.

Tribal dance

Normally lunch is taken at Outspan Hotel – perhaps with a display of Kikuyu dancing in the compound – followed by the drive to Treetops along a dirt road, with armed escort for the final short stretch on foot.

Treetops rates as Africa's best-known safari hotel, with historical fame. Here Queen Elizabeth II acceded to the throne on the death of her father in 1952.

GAME PARKS

Despite its setting, Treetops has a bar, dining room, lounges and tiny rustic bedrooms with shared facilities. Suitcases are left at the Outspan Hotel, and guests make do with living out of flight bags. Dinner is served at Treetops. The following morning, after wake-up tea or coffee, visitors return to Outspan Hotel for a regular cooked breakfast.

Perched 40 feet high amid the branches of giant Cape Chestnut trees, guests have a bird's-eye view over the waterholes which are floodlit all night by artificial moons.

Meanwhile, animals start to arrive during the afternoon. Usually the first are waterbuck, bushbuck and warthog. At teatime on the rooftop observation platform, baboons, glossy blue starlings and weaver birds come to share the crumbs. Then as evening approaches, buffalo, rhino, elephant and families of giant forest hog appear at the waterhole.

Most visitors continue to watch the ever-changing show until past midnight.

Wildlife includes Red Duiker, Suni, Bushbuck, Leopard, Colobus Monkey, Bush Pig, Clawless Otter, Eland, Serval, Bongo, Rhino, Lion, Elephant.

Birdlife includes Francolin, Hill Chat, White-naped Raven, Scarlet-tufted Malachite Sunbird.

Also in the Aberdare National Park are two other hotels of similar design to Treetops: the Mountain Lodge, and The Ark (built like the upswept bows of the biblical sanctuary designed by Noah).

4.7 Lakes Baringo and Bogoria

These two neighbouring lakes are located 150 miles north of Nairobi. Described by explorers as 'the most beautiful view in Africa', Lake Bogoria is a National Reserve with shorelines of boiling geysers – a reminder of the volcanic origins of the Great Rift Valley.

The lake is alkaline, and is therefore a preferred habitat for shimmering thousands of lesser flamingo. The Reserve is not rich in game, but there's good chance of seeing the Greater Kudu, and uncommon antelopes such as the Klipspringer and Chanler's Reedbuck.

Just a short distance north of Bogoria is **Lake Baringo.** On the lake shores the Lake Baringo Country Club Hotel has lovely gardens and a swimming pool.

Paradise for twitchers

Birdlife in the area is some of the most varied and concentrated in Kenya, with over 400 species recorded. Bird viewing by boat or on foot is often accompanied by the club's resident ornithologist. Hippo and crocodiles are plentiful.

Birdlife includes largest nesting colony of Goliath Herons, Verreaux' Eagle, Hemprich's Hornbill, Curly-crested Helmet Shrike and the rare Bristle-crowned Starling.

4.8 Lake Nakuru and Nyahururu

This 72-sq-mile game reserve was first established as a bird sanctuary in 1960, and became a national park in 1967. The shallow alkaline lake produces a blue-green algae which is the staple food of enormous flocks of Lesser Flamingoes, found only in the Rift Valley.

The Greater Flamingoes choose an alternative diet of crustaceans. Several hundred other bird species are recorded.

Down past some strange cactus-like trees to the lakeside, you can walk on the soda mud for a closer colour picture of the flamingoes and egrets. Other species include Cape Widgeon, Maccoa Duck, African Hoopoe, Drongo and Cuckoo.

Also look for Hippos, the Bohor Reedbuck and the Long-eared Leaf-nosed Bat. The National Park also contains the country's first Rhino Sanctuary.

Lake Nakuru Lodge offers superb views over the plains and towards the lake, while game wanders freely nearby.

The town of Nakuru, fourth largest in Kenya, is located about 100 miles from Nairobi, in a rich farming area. Another 44-mile drive northeast, just across the equator is Thomson's Falls, renamed Nyahururu. A refreshment stop is usually made here, en route to or from the Samburu Game Reserve.

The Falls were originally named by a Scotsman, Joseph Thomson, who in 1883 was the first European to explore through to Lake Victoria.

If you cannot locate any specimens of the three-horned chameleon, enterprising locals can usually produce one which you can photograph at a price. The Falls themselves are best after heavy rain.

4.9 Lake Naivasha

Outward bound from Nairobi, heading northwest up the Rift Valley towards Nakuru along the A104 Uplands road, a left turning along B3 highway leads towards Narok and the Maasai Mara Game Reserve. Otherwise keep straight on, passing 9,109-ft Mount Langonot on the left – an extinct volcano, but still steaming.

Halfway between Nairobi and Lake Nakuru is the freshwater Lake Naivasha, fringed with papyrus and and blue water lilies, and fabulously rich in birdlife. This must rank among the loveliest of the eight lakes of the Rift Valley. At 6,200 ft altitude it's also the highest of the lakes, 43 sq miles in area.

Little more than an hour's drive from Nairobi, a visit to Lake Naivasha makes a feasible whole-day excursion from the capital, to include a tour of the local vineyards and a visit to the Elmenteita Weavers to watch spinning and weaving activities.

The peaceful and relaxing hotel, shaded by spreading acacias, is situated close to the lake shore. The lawn is a landing-place for ibis and marabou storks, wagtails, swallows and swifts, while superb glossy starlings forage on the tables for crumbs. A stroll down to the lake edge gives ample opportunity to watch and film herons, wading birds with matchstick legs, black-winged stilt or avocet. Water fowl are plentiful on the lakeside, and in old tree branches sticking out of the water. On islands of floating vegetation are breeding colonies of pelicans and cormorants.

Crescent Island

Highly recommended is to take the 10-minute boat trip to Crescent Island, and to be collected at an agreed time. The boat ride also gives the chance of seeing some of the resident hippos. Along the island's curved shoreline are plentiful photo opportunities for cormorants, divers, herons, coots, egrets, blacksmith plovers or spur-winged plovers.

Other notable species include Fish Eagles, Ospreys, Purple Gallinules, Black Crakes, Red-knobbed Coots and African Marsh Harriers. The island also is tenanted by some gazelle and waterbuck. A tripod and long-focus lens are the best equipment, shooting at fast speed and wide aperture to give shallow depth of field.

Hell's Gate

Eight miles south of the lake, the Hell's Gate National Park through the Njorowa gorge is home to herds of plains game – giraffe, zebra, impala, eland, Grant's and Thomson's gazelle – but none of the big predators. Natural hot steam jets are a reminder of the proximity of volcanic Mount Longonot. In this region is the Olkaria Geothermal Area, where electric power is generated from an underground source that delivers high-pressure water at around 300° C. The target is to supply up to half of Kenya's energy needs – effectively harnessing the volcano.

4.10 Maasai Mara

Considered to be Kenya's leading Game Reserve, the Maasai Mara lies 170 miles west of Nairobi, with its western boundary common with Tanzania's Serengeti. At around 5,200-ft altitude the reserve features grassy plains, scrub, acacia woodland and lush riverine forest.

From May or June each year over two million zebra, wildebeest and accompanying predators surge across the Tanzanian border to the Maasai Mara in their quest for fresh pastures. This awe-inspiring sight goes into reverse in November or December when the herds return to the Serengeti.

In the Maasai Mara you can see the black-maned lion for which the reserve is famous, besides the other members of the Big Five. There are thousands of topi, and wallowing hippos and crocodiles.

On the drive from Nairobi via Narok, the route passes from Kikuyu to Maasai country. Kikuyu fence their pieces of land or smallholdings on which they grow enough to provide a surplus to sell. In contrast, the Maasai follow their herdsman tradition of not dividing or fencing their country.

Balloon safari

The Reserve is well equipped with Lodges and tented camps, and there is a wide range of game trails. In the heart of the Reserve is Keekorok Lodge, offering great views towards the Mara Plains. For added excitement, balloon flights are operated from here. Similar facilities are offered across the border in Tanzania.

The balloons take off in the cool early morning, with a Land Rover as chase vehicle. The going price includes a champagne picnic breakfast, which passes the time while the chase crew is packing up the balloon for the return by surface. Earthlings have a dining-room breakfast in the normal way.

After the relative boredom of other forms of air travel, a game-viewing balloon flight must rate among the great memories of a lifetime. Your camera can capture the massive solidity of a lone elephant, stuffing himself with victuals and taking no notice of the balloon floating above. Over a waterhole you watch a vast herd of buffalo; and then a peaceful giraffe family of three, standing motionless beside a bush.

All these vignettes can rate among the highlights of a Kenyan safari. Meanwhile the regular game-viewing drives can be equally packed with excitement.

Here's a listing of animals seen on a typical morning's drive: zebra, waterbuck, wildebeest, Thomson's gazelle, buffalo, hartebeest, hippos, helmeted guinea fowl, lion (one male on his own, and then a pride), elephants, topi, vultures, impala, black-breasted bustard, cheetah (one moving and then a female in the shade), hare, lilac-breasted roller, Grant's gazelle, Maasai ostrich, secretary birds, giraffe, wart hogs, hyena and seven elephants with baby. Good viewing!

4.11 Samburu

Two hundred miles from Nairobi, and fifty miles north of Mount Kenya, is the Samburu National Reserve. In a sandy, semi-desert region of acacia woodland, bush and scrub, the sluggish Ewaso Nyiro River brings rich life to the riverine woodland of doum palm. Established in 1963 to protect the large numbers and great variety of wildlife species, the effective boundaries were later extended by the creation of two adjoining Reserves – Shaba and Buffalo Springs. Between them, the trio comprise over 200 square miles of protected area. Shaba National Reserve was the home for many years of author Joy Adamson.

On the 160-mile journey to Samburu from the Aberdares direction, the route passes many coffee plantations. Peas and potatoes are often grown between fence and road. There are good crops of wheat and barley, and large herds of cows in good condition.

Snow-capped 17,057-ft Mount Kenya remains visible for a long time. A halt is usually made at a much photographed Equator sign at Nanyuki. Sometimes the road altitude is at 9,000 ft, and then drops to 6,000 ft.

Extinct volcanoes

The wild and rugged northern region, with its mountain ranges and extinct volcanoes, comprises more than half of Kenya, and borders the Sudan, Ethiopia and Somalia. Nomads follow their traditional way of life, herding cattle, goats and camels.

In contrast, the Samburu Reserve is like an oasis, with the spectacular mountains of the Mathews Range rising to the north. Several well-established Lodges are located along the river banks, blending with the surroundings. The attractive and comfortable Samburu Lodge, built of local stone and mountain cedar, offers accommodation either in a modern wing or in spacious rustic chalets. Water is heated by solar power.

Feeding time

There's an open air lounge by the Crocodile Bar, where crocodiles can be viewed daily at feeding time, as well as a swimming pool where guests can relax. Hippos and elephants drink and bathe in the river. On the opposite bank, lion and leopard are attracted nightly by floodlit bait tied to an angled tree-trunk.

Free food is also an attraction to other local residents. Varied birds come regularly to open-air dining areas in search of crumbs. Everybody's favourite is the Superb Glossy Starling – blue and orange and cheeky. Watch your breakfast! Garden monkeys are expert in grabbing pineapple slices from your plate.

On game-viewing drives, Samburu is one of the few places to see the fuzzy-eared Grevy's zebra, Beisa oryx, reticulated giraffe and the graceful gerenuk (the giraffe-necked gazelle which stands on its hind legs to feed on prickly bushes and trees).

Including migrants, well over 300 bird species have been recorded – from the prolific colonies of weaver birds, to hornbills, vulturine guineafowl, Bateleur eagles and the blue-shanked Somali ostrich.

More photo opportunities are offered by local Samburu tribesmen who give dramatic dance performances, with much chanting and jumping around.

Most visitors leave Samburu with regret.

Chapter Five

Safari into Tanzania

While Nairobi, Kenya, is the traditional starting-point for East African tours, many of the best game-viewing areas are across the border in northern Tanzania.

The best-known park is Serengeti – 5,000 square miles with some of the world's greatest herds of plains animals: wildebeest, gazelle, zebra, eland, stalked by lion, leopard and cheetah predators.

Adjoining Serengeti is the Ngorongoro Crater. Land Rovers descend the 2,000 ft crater wall for viewing of more wildlife herds and the 'Big Five' – elephant, rhino, lion, leopard and buffalo.

Lake Manyara is famed for birdlife, especially flamingoes and pelicans. A curiosity is that local lions spend leisure time dozing in upper branches of trees.

The best seasons for game photography are November to March, and June to October.

Travellers who intend to visit Tanzania or to take an excursion to Zanzibar must have a Tanzanian Visitors Visa costing £38 in UK or $50 at the border.

5.1 Background to Tanzania

Formerly called Tanganyika, the United Republic of Tanzania includes the islands of Mafia, Pemba and Zanzibar. This vast country is four times the size of Britain or twice that of California. Independence dates from 1961, followed three years later by the merger with Zanzibar.

To the north Tanzania is bounded by Kenya, Lake Victoria and Uganda; to the south by Zambia, Malawi and Mozambique.

Within its borders lie Africa's highest mountain (Mount Kilimanjaro), the world's largest game reserve

(Selous) and the greatest concentration of wildlife to be found anywhere.

Three great rivers – the Nile, Congo and Zambezi – are fed by the Tanzanian watershed.

Incredibly, it means that rainfall over Tanzania can ultimately flow into either the Mediterranean, the Atlantic or the Indian Ocean.

5.2 Arusha

The principal town of Northern Tanzania, Arusha is an old trading post, lying exactly half way between Cairo and the Cape. Due south of Nairobi, it's an easy 170-mile journey along highway A104; or from the east along A23 from Mombasa through Voi and Moshi.

The dominating peak of Kilimanjaro rises above the snowline to 19,340-ft Mount Kibo. An ascent normally requires five days – three days up, two down. The best months for the climb are January, February, September and October – avoiding the rains of April and May. The encircling rain forest ensures fertility to lower-lying areas where coffee, bananas and maize are cultivated.

There are tourist hotels in Arusha, and recent developments in the region include high-grade farm accommodation in guesthouse style.

Shops in Arusha open from 08.30 to 17.00 hrs Monday to Saturday. There are very few shopping opportunities whilst out on safari, except for purchase of curios.

Banking hours are 08.30-12.30 Monday to Friday; 08.30-11.30 Saturday. Local currency is the Tanzania Shilling, but US Dollars and Travellers Cheques are widely accepted.

Arusha National Park

This mountainous Park, 20 miles northwest of Arusha past coffee-growing farms, ranges from an altitude of between 5,000 and 15,000 ft. Only 53 sq miles in size, it incorporates three distinct areas: the Ngurdoto Crater, Momella and Mount Meru.

The Park encompasses a great variety of scenery, from lakes and waterfalls to primeval forest on the slopes of Mount Meru.

Extinct for the past quarter-million years, Ngurdoto was a subsidiary vent of the Meru volcano. The north side blew out, releasing ash, lava and mud deposits in which the Momella Lakes eventually formed, to mirror the snows of Kilimanjaro in their waters.

There is no visitor access into the Ngurdoto Crater – partly because of impassable swamps, but also to ensure that there is nil disturbance from man. From viewpoints on the rim, the resident animals can be seen a thousand feet below.

Wildlife includes Elephant, Buffalo, Red Forest Duiker, Waterbuck, Hippo, Warthog, Bohor Reedbuck and rare black and white Colobus Monkeys. There are occasional Leopard, but no Lion.

Bird life is abundant, with many northern migrants that fly in to avoid the European winter.

5.3 Tarangire National Park

Located 60 miles from Arusha, and south of Lake Manyara, the Tarangire River is the only source of water in the 525-sq-mile reserve and therefore attracts an abundance of game and birdlife.

Scattered baobab trees alternate with open acacia woodland. October to May is the best period for bird watchers.

Wildlife includes Elephant, Rhinoceros, Buffalo, Oryx, Gerenuk, Zebra, Jackal, Bohur Reedbuck, Coke's Hartebeeste and Bushbuck.

Birdlife includes Maasai Ostrich, Pink-backed Pelican, Steppe Buzzard, Hooded Vulture, Crowned Crane, Pied Kingfisher, Crombee, Green Wood Hoopoe, Red-billed Hornbill and the Laughing Dove.

5.4 Lake Manyara National Park

Established in 1960, Lake Manyara National Park at 3,000-ft altitude is spread below precipitous cliffs in the Great Rift Valley, about 80 miles from Arusha. Here the Rift Valley has no eastern wall and the lake lies in a flat depression which stretches away to the south and east.

Within a compact area of only 123 sq miles the terrain is extremely diverse, with a variety of habitats:

● **Ground water forest** at the park entrance is fed by streams which gush from the volcanic rock – an area ideal for elephant, rhino and zebra;

- **Mixed woodland**, the home of elephant, rhino, impala, giraffe and zebra;
- **Dry thicket vegetation** consisting of deciduous trees and large baobabs, beloved of the elephant;
- **Maji Moto** in the south of the Park, with hot springs which are a favourite feeding ground of innumerable birds;
- **Alkaline grassland** along the lake shore.

Tree-climbers

Manyara is famous for its lions and leopards who climb trees, relaxing amid branches of acacias. The explanation for this habit is uncertain – perhaps to avoid the flies, or to catch a cooling breeze. It's a favourite subject for wildlife photographers.

Wildlife includes Elephant, Buffalo, Leopard, Hippopotamus, Olive Baboon, Zebra, Warthog and the Tree-climbing Lion.

Birdlife includes Lesser Flamingo, Maccoa Duck, White-backed Duck, Pygmy Goose, Chestnut-banded Sand Plover, Palm Nut Vulture, Ayres' and Crowned Hawk Eagles.

5.5 Ngorongoro Crater

Ngorongoro is the largest unbroken, unflooded volcanic caldera in the world. It lies 120 miles or 4 hours' drive west of Arusha. The average height of the rim is 7,600 feet.

Descent to the crater floor, 2,000 feet below, is permitted only to locally based four wheel drive vehicles. Any other Land Rovers must be accompanied by a licensed guide.

The view from the rim is spectacular. About eleven miles wide, the crater features mainly open grassy plains with a small soda lake, two swamps, acacia woodlands and several fresh water springs which attract permanent animal life.

The Maasai

Ngorongoro Crater is not a national park, but a conservation area for the benefit both of the Maasai herdsmen and the wild animals.

No farming development is permitted, but the local Maasai follow their traditional lifestyle, grazing their cattle within the area without disturbance to the resident wildlife.

This unique World Heritage Site is the home of rhino, elephant, prides of lion and more than 14,000 wildebeest, 5,000 zebra and hundreds of gazelle.

Bird life is also rich with more than 350 species identified.

Lodges on the crater rim command sweeping views from their altitudes of around 8000 ft. The nights can be cold. Some of the rooms are centrally heated, and warm clothing is recommended.

Wildlife includes Elephant, Lion, Black Rhinoceros, Hippopotamus, Buffalo, Cheetah, Eland, Grant's and Thomson's Gazelles, Common Zebra, Spotted Hyena, Wildebeest, Hunting Dog and an occasional Leopard.

Birdlife includes Lammergeyer, Verreaux's Eagle, Egyptian Vulture, Ostrich, Pelican, Rosy-breasted Longclaw, Lesser and Greater Flamingo and European Black Stork.

5.6 Olduvai Gorge

Olduvai forms part of the Serengeti ecosystem, and has been called the Cradle of Mankind.

The gorge, carved by water action, exposes successive fossil-bed layers that were formed up to more than three million years ago. Scientists can study the fossilized remains of long-extinct animals in their identifiable time sequences.

In this remote and parched canyon Dr Louis Leakey and his wife Mary (parents of Dr. Richard Leakey who later directed the Kenya Wildlife Service) found the skull of Nutcracker Man.

He was so called because of huge teeth that suggested a diet of coarse vegetables. These hominoid remains were over 1,750,000 years old.

Since this discovery in 1959, even earlier discoveries have been made, including hominoid and animal footprints which were solidified in volcanic ash over three million years ago – found by Mrs Mary Leakey at Laetoli in 1979. These sites in the Olduvai Gorge lend weight to the theory that homo sapiens originated in Africa.

A small museum at the Visitor Centre explains the scientific significance of these finds, and describes the work which continues in the area.

5.7 Serengeti National Park

Second largest of Tanzania's parks, after Selous, the Serengeti is the sanctuary with the greatest concentration of wildlife on earth. It lies between the Ngorongoro highlands and the Kenyan border, where it extends into the Maasai Mara Game Reserve.

Several lodges and camps are located in different areas of the Serengeti. They are all good bases for viewing the wildlife of this magnificent park.

The main features of Serengeti are the open grassland plains in the south, the scattered acacia savannah in the central area, a more densely wooded hilly region in the north and along the Mara River, and the black clay plains and mountains of the western corridor towards Lake Victoria. Outcrops of granite rock – kopjes – provide shade and protection to numerous creatures.

The great migrations

The Serengeti is world famed for the annual migration of millions of animals. Depending on the rainy seasons, in May and June every year a million wildebeest and zebra commute from their normal grazing territory in the south, to the permanent water corridor of the west and north; then return again in November or December when the southern grass turns green again.

This migration of enormous herds six to eight abreast, several miles long, has become one of the most remarkable and awe-inspiring sights in East Africa. The herds are closely followed by predators.

Wildlife includes Wildebeest, Zebra, Grant's Gazelle, Topi, Buffalo, Jackal, Striped Hyena, Black-faced Vervet Monkey, Cheetah, Oribi, Bush Pig and Lion.

Birdlife includes Grey-breasted Spurfowl, Brown-chested Wattled Plover, Rufous-tailed Weaver, Little Tawny Pipit, Schalow's Turaco, and Red-throated Tit.

5.8 Zanzibar

A popular overnight excursion from Kenyan resorts is to the clove-scented coral island of Zanzibar, reached by a one-hour flight from Mombasa. A yellow fever certificate and a visa are required, and airport taxes amount to US $45 per person. Located 20 miles from the mainland, due north of Dar Es Salaam, 640-sq-mile

TANZANIA

Zanzibar rates high among the world's most beautiful and historic islands. *See map on page 48.*

Among the earliest visitors were Egyptians, Chinese and Malays. The island was settled around 1,000 AD by Africans who later mixed with traders from the Persian Gulf – Arab, Persian and Indian. From 1499 Zanzibar came under Portuguese control, following a visit by the explorer Vasco da Gama. In turn, Arabs ruled here from 1698 onwards, and used Zanzibar as the main base for their rich trade in slaves and ivory.

In 1832 the Sultan of Muscat made Zanzibar the capital of his dominions, which included much of the East African coast. The production of cloves, which originated in the East Indies, was introduced to Zanzibar and the sister island of Pemba by the first Arab Sultan. Soon the two islands became the world's principal source of clove production. Even today they account for 80% of the world supply. Zanzibar also has lush plantations of nutmegs, cinnamon, cocoa and coconut, and you can scent their presence everywhere.

The slave trade was finally abolished in 1873, though it still continued illegally for another 25 years. The sultanate became a British Protectorate in 1890, with independence in 1964. From Zanzibar the great 19th-century African explorers – Burton, Speke, Grant and Livingstone – departed on their journeys into the interior. Near the dhow harbour where slaves were unloaded is Livingstone House, where the explorer lived while planning his last expedition in 1866.

Zanzibar's historic exposure to different cultures has left its mark on both the people and the architecture. The population is 80% of African descent, 10% Arab, 7% Indian. Reflecting the considerable Arab influence, most of the islanders are Sunni Moslems. Likewise in Zanzibar town dazzling white Arab houses are closely packed along narrow lanes, with heavy brass-studded wooden doors to ensure privacy. Traditional Arab skill in silver, copper and leather still flourishes.

Among the sites to visit are the ruins of Marahubi Palace, built about 4 miles out of town for the harem of Sultan Bargash who ruled from 1870 till 1888. The Sultan's town palace is located on the seafront in town, and is now named the People's Palace. Adjoining the Arab fort close by is the Beit el Ajaib – House of Wonders – with beautifully carved Arab doors, marble floors and silver decorations.

Chapter Six

A taste of Zimbabwe

6.1 Introduction

Three times the size of England, Zimbabwe is one of Africa's most enlightened states for wildlife protection. Altogether, Zimbabwe's twentyfive National Parks cover around 14 percent of the country. Hwange, the largest reserve, is about the size of Belgium.

Zimbabwe's tourism future is based on preservation of the natural grandeur of the scenery, coupled with the pleasure of seeing wildlife in its natural environment. Game wardens act vigorously against poachers, though it's an uphill battle to protect the rhino. Some large estates, such as Pamuzinda Safari Lodge, operate as private game reserves where a handful of visitors can view the wildlife in tranquillity.

Zimbabwe can offer a variety of travel experiences which make African journeys so memorable – beautiful climate, good hotels, fabulous scenery and game viewing. The tourism industry is well run, with top-rate facilities everywhere.

The flourishing modern capital, Harare (formerly Salisbury), is a garden city where three major 5-star hotels offer service that can rival anything in Africa. It's a venue for prestigious international Conferences.

The country's greatest prosperity comes from farms which produce some of the world's finest Virginia flue-cured tobacco. In Harare, visitors may freely enter the tobacco auction floors – a fascinating sight from Easter till September, when the crop is sold for export.

Zimbabwe is a rock-hound's paradise, with innumerable varieties of semi-precious stones on sale and manufactured into jewellery. Display boxes of different stones make a popular tourist purchase; or one can choose from baskets of polished stone eggs of all sizes.

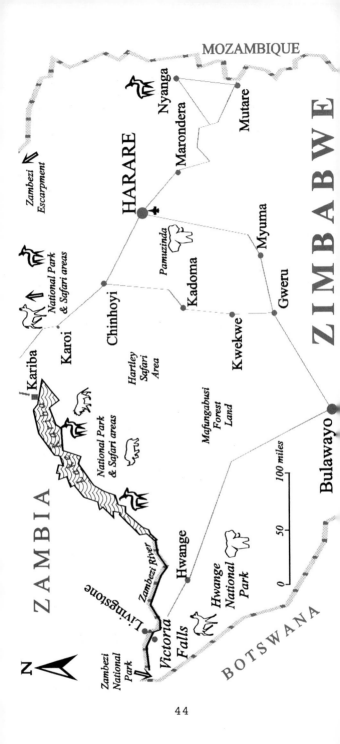

Wood and soapstone carving

Stone sculpture has been a boom artistic industry in recent decades, with many works of art-gallery quality. The best pieces are collectors' items, while the larger works are bought by banks and company headquarters to lend elegance to their premises. Harare's National Art Gallery has a superb collection.

Climate

The best time for game-viewing is during the dry 'winter' months from May until September – beautiful months of cloudless skies, with comfortable temperatures.

October and November are the hottest, when even the locally-born citizens droop with the heat. But those two months are the unsurpassable best for game-viewing, when the grass is wilted, and the game easy to spot.

Rainy season is December till March, when the grass and the crops grow tall and even elephants become invisible. But that's when the Victoria Falls are at their most awesome best.

6.2 Victoria Falls

The Victoria Falls rate as Africa's greatest sightseeing highlight, with the mile-wide Zambezi River plunging over a 300-ft cliff. At tail-end of the rains, 75 million gallons a minute thunder down. The towering curtain of spray is a hindrance to shutterbugs, who can get pictures easier during the dry season, when the flow steadily subsides to a mere November trickle of four million gallons each minute.

Sightseeing includes scenic drives to all the main vantage points: the Eastern Cataract, the Devil's Cataract, and the fantastic gorges that carry away the boiling water. You can walk through the Rain Forest created by the perpetual spray, following footpaths that open onto dramatic viewpoints of the gorge.

A 'Sundowner' launch cruise on the Zambezi with open bar offers the chance of seeing hippo or crocodile, especially during the dry season. Otherwise, tourists can always visit the Spencer Creek Crocodile Farm which has 2,000 reptiles of varying sizes to inspect.

A major thrill is a 15-minute joy-ride over the Falls by helicopter or twin-engined aircraft. The trip is billed as the "Flight of the Angels", following Livingstone's comment when he saw the Falls: "Scenes so lovely must have been gazed upon by angels in their flight".

The most famous accommodation is the historic Victoria Falls Hotel, with a grandstand view of "The Smoke that Thunders". Built in 1904, the hotel has kept its Edwardian colonial atmosphere with long, rambling corridors, spacious bedrooms and excellent service, while everything within has been modernised.

Local displays of traditional African dancing show you the colourful life that David Livingstone first saw when he explored the region in 1855. Little has changed since then, except for construction of access-roads to serve the full tourist range of hotels, camp-sites, serviced chalets and cottages.

The town of Livingstone itself is across the border in Zambia, linked by a dramatic road and rail bridge across the gorge which marks the frontier. For the thrill of a lifetime, some visitors go bungee-jumping off the bridge!

A popular attraction is the Falls Craft Village, where local craftsmen do traditional wood-carving, make musical instruments and even operate a primitive forge. The Village demonstrates the life-styles of six ethnic groups, with curios for sale.

6.3 Private game-viewing

Only an hour's drive from Harare through interesting farming country is Pamuzinda Safari Lodge, located within a private 5,000-acre reserve which is home to a large variety of wildlife. A check-list features 120 varieties of birds and 30 mammals from lion and Cape buffalo to waterbuck and aardvark. This was the favourite hunting ground of Frederick Courteney Selous, a famous 19th-century hunter and pioneer.

The Mupfure River where Selous and his entourage camped is now peacefully explored in canoes, or with a knowledgeable game guide on foot, on horseback or in a Land Rover.

These activities provide ideal game spotting and photo opportunities. Several young elephants have been reintroduced to the reserve and are spotted regularly from the Lodge and on game drives.

Guests can also absorb some of the rich history of the area known as 'The Royal Meeting Place'.

Chapter Seven
The Mombasa coast

7.1 Introduction

For combined safari and beach holidays, the Indian Ocean offers 300 miles of utterly perfect coastline: powder-fine sands, backed by groves of softly-rustling coconut palms. There are flowers everywhere: oleander, frangipani, hibiscus and bougainvillaea.

About half a mile offshore, a coral reef runs almost the entire length of the Kenya coast, creating lagoons of crystal-clear water between coral headlands. The shoreline is broken by occasional river creeks. Water temperatures stay in the eighties Fahrenheit year-round.

The reefs themselves enclose a goggle-swimmer's paradise, with fantastically-coloured shells easily seen in the sparkling waters. From most hotels you can spend enthralling hours in a glass bottom boat at the coral reef, where the marine world is as interest-packed as any Kenyan game reserve.

Shoals of multi-coloured and striped tropical fish dart amid the fantastic mushroom shapes and fronded branches of the coral. Every few seconds, another brilliant fish catches the eye, as it weaves amid this paradise of colour.

From tiny coastal hamlets, African fishermen use dug-out boats with outriggers. They return with good hauls of oysters, scampi, crayfish, octopus, rock-cod and kingfish. If you want to try your hand at big-game fishing, there's prospect of sailfish or marlin in deep water beyond the reef.

Excellent beach hotels are located a few miles outside Mombasa both north and south, and at peaceful locations further along the coast north to Malindi. They are all laid out in best tropical paradise tradition, often with palm-thatch roofing.

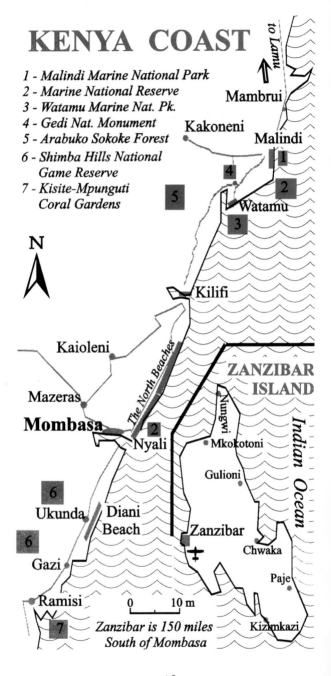

KENYA COAST

1 - Malindi Marine National Park
2 - Marine National Reserve
3 - Watamu Marine Nat. Pk.
4 - Gedi Nat. Monument
5 - Arabuko Sokoke Forest
6 - Shimba Hills National
    Game Reserve
7 - Kisite-Mpunguti
    Coral Gardens

to Lamu

Mambrui

Kakoneni

Malindi

1

2

Watamu

3

4

5

N

Kilifi

Kaioleni

The North Beaches

ZANZIBAR
ISLAND

Mazeras

Mombasa

2

Nyali

Nungwi

Mkokotoni

Gulioni

Indian Ocean

6

Ukunda

Diani
Beach

Zanzibar

Chwaka

6

Gazi

Paje

Ramisi

0   10 m

Kizimkazi

7

*Zanzibar is 150 miles
South of Mombasa*

Victoria Falls

Mombasa

Maasai children

A traditional dhow

Some hotels are designed in African village style, with thatched rondavels set among lush gardens. You can swing like a carefree beachcomber in a hammock strung between the trees, or just drift across the pool on an air-mattress, propelled by the Indian Ocean breezes. When the going gets tough, you can freshen with a tall Tusker beer. It all makes a leisured contrast to the movement and excitement of a game safari.

Even if you have planned to spend all your holiday at the beach, you can still make a local reservation for a mini-safari or sightseeing trip: all day or overnight to the Shimba Hills Reserve, for instance; overnight at Zanzibar island; Tsavo East in a day, or a one- or two-night package. Even a trip by air to Amboseli and Mt Kilimanjaro is possible. There are numerous options. Simply see your representative for details.

7.2 Mombasa

Kenya's second city with nearly a million inhabitants is the largest port along the Indian Ocean coast after South Africa's Durban. A crowded island of under five square miles, Mombasa is linked to the mainland by several causeways, bridges and ferries.

Thanks to its excellent position as a trading centre, approached through a handy gap in the barrier reef and providing safe anchorage for sailing vessels, Mombasa has a rich history. The island and its harbour was known to the Greeks in the first century AD.

The whole coast was opened up by Persian and Arab merchants mainly between 1100 and 1300 AD and again in the 15th century. Trading shipments between Africa and the Middle East were handled by the classic Arab dhows – coasting vessels used throughout the Red Sea and Persian Gulf.

Generally the lateen-rigged dhows were about 150 to 200 tons, originally fitted with very large triangular sails made of matting, but later of cotton. If the wind failed for the last sheltered mile or two across the harbour, the crews heaved at clumsy oars to bring in their ships to shore.

From Mombasa's Dhow Harbour, the Arab captains based their business on the export of ivory, gold, leopard skins, rhino horn and slaves from the interior. That trading pattern no longer operates, except possibly for illegal smuggling of animal trophies.

Any remaining commercial dhows are now equipped with diesel engines, though they still keep their picturesque appearance. A few dhows operate up and down the coast, carrying varied cargoes of flour, fish, copra, Coca-Cola. Occasionally a larger dhow sails in from the Gulf, laden with Persian carpets.

Otherwise, the traditional vessels have now switched into tourist business, featuring day trips along the coast and through the mangrove forests of tidal creeks. A tranquil day, highly recommended!

The Portuguese arrive

The best-known early visitor from Europe was the Portuguese navigator, Vasco da Gama, who arrived in 1498. Mombasa gave him an unfriendly reception, leading the explorer to establish better relations at Malindi.

A Portuguese fleet came back to Mombasa in 1505 for a one-sided combat of arrows versus gunpowder. The Portuguese looted and burned the city, and gained trading control of the coast for the next 200 years. But the basic conflict erupted every few years, with the Portuguese wrecking and looting Mombasa five times during the 16th century. Finally the Portuguese settled in to Mombasa themselves, transferring from their main base at Malindi.

The principal Portuguese contribution to the city was the Italian-designed pink-walled Fort Jesus on the north side of the island. It was completed in 1593 on a five-pointed star ground plan that exposed would-be attackers to crossfire from the bastions. Elderly cannon still dominate the Dhow Harbour while the massive 50-ft ramparts overlook the Arab-style Old Town.

Open 8.30-19.00 hrs daily, a small museum in the former barracks focusses on the Swahili culture of the Kenya coast. Also on display are items salvaged from a Portuguese frigate, sunk at the harbour entrance in 1697 by gunfire from the Omani Arabs who were besieging the fortress. The ship was bringing food and reinforcements, in an attempt to raise a siege which lasted 33 months.

Arab control

When the Arabs finally entered the fort, only 15 survivors remained from the fort's original population of 2,000, mostly carried off by starvation and plague.

That event marked the end of Portuguese domination of the East Africa coast, and they departed for good in 1720.

Buildings in the Old Town are mainly 19th century, though the narrow streets, alleys and courtyards follow the centuries'-old layout of a traditional Arab-city maze. Along the Ndia Kuu Road, nearest to Fort Jesus, curio and souvenir shops clamour for attention. There are silk dealers, spice merchants, goldsmiths and perfumiers.

Of more architectural interest are the carved balconies, heavy doors and barred windows of the solid coral-rock houses occupied by Asian and Arab families. In this area, on Bachawy Road, is the Mandhry Mosque dating from 1570 – easily picked out by its tilted minaret.

Ethnic diversity

Mombasa is a city of ethnic and religious diversity, with around 50 mosques, and Anglican and Roman Catholic churches. Numerous Hindu and Jain Temples are a reminder of the economic success of the Asian community, descended both from Indian traders and craftsmen, and from the railway contract workers who arrived in East Africa in the 1890's. The gleaming white-marble Jain Temple on Langoni Road was completed in wedding-cake style only 30-odd years ago. Most of the mosques and temples are open to visitors who follow the normal etiquette of modest dress and the removal of shoes.

Digo Road marks the boundary between the old and the modern city. The principal market place is worth visiting for its colourful displays of tropical fruit, while neighbouring stores specialise in spices, tea and coffee. Biashara Street is famed for its brilliant range of *kanga* cotton fabric designs.

One-day sightseeing

Most holidaymakers at the coastal resorts make a one-day visit to Mombasa – enough to see the main sights, cross back to the mainland to see the Akamba wood carvers at work and then return to the centre with time for shopping. Another option is to board a traditional Arab dhow to explore Tudor Creek. At the end of the creek there is a novel floating market where you can bargain for handicrafts.

Apart from this sightseeing potential, Mombasa is not a tourist town. The hotels are designed more for business travellers. Much of the nightlife caters for the more urgent needs of lonely sailors.

Moi Avenue

The principal dual carriageway is Moi Avenue (the former Kilindini Road) which cuts across the island between Old Town and the docks and industrial area.

Along Moi Avenue are banks, travel agencies, curio stands, the Castle Hotel and the archways formed by four jumbo-sized aluminium elephant tusks, erected in 1953 to mark the coronation of Queen Elizabeth II. Close by this well-known landmark is the Information Bureau (Mon-Fri 8-12 and 14-16.30 hrs; Sat 8-12 hrs).

From Mombasa island, the Makupa Causeway leads to the airport and is also the road and rail route to Nairobi. From the Likoni Ferry a surfaced highway stretches seventy miles south to the Tanzanian border. The Nyali Bridge gives access to the north coast resorts.

7.3 South coast

The principal holiday location south of Mombasa is Diani Beach, where some two dozen hotels, lodges and self-catering developments are spread along the 7-mile stretch of powder-fine sand.

Apart from all the standard beach and watersport facilities, the main hotels feature evening barbecues, live bands, discos, video wildlife films and African tribal dances.

Parallel to Diani Beach, just a few miles inland, are the Shimba Hills where visitors can sample a one-day safari to the National Reserve, with chance of seeing elephant and roan and sable antelope. *See page 28.*

Thirty miles further south – past sugar-cane and coconut plantations – is Shimoni, named from the Swahili word for the coral caves where slaves were penned while awaiting shipment. Today the caves house bats.

Shimoni itself is a Mecca for big game fishermen, angling for marlin and shark.

South of Wasini Island is the Kisite Mpunguti Marine National Park, which offers ideal snorkelling and scuba potential with extensive coral gardens and tropical fish to see.

7.4 North coast

With easy access from Mombasa across Tudor Creek, the Nyali Bridge leads to the north coast beaches which start at Nyali garden suburb. Besides all the usual land and water sports at the beach hotels, Nyali features an 18-hole golf course, the Bamburi Nature Trail and the Mamba Crocodile Village. Worth a special visit!

Running northwards, the B8 highway serves hotels that spread along the main beach developments. Twelve miles north is Mtwapwa Creek, starting point for a typical day trip aboard an old Arab dhow which sails along the coast whilst the crew check their fish traps. Passengers can help with the work, or steer the boat.

Back at Mtwapwa, after lunch the dhow cruises up the narrow and picturesque creek to view the exotic flora and rich birdlife typical of all the coastal mangrove stands. Some trips include a visit to Kenya Marineland's big sea water Aquarium and Snake Park; and – depending on the agency package – there may be bonus entertainment by fire eaters, Maasai and limbo dancers.

Continuing 25 miles further north past sisal plantations, the road reaches Kilifi Creek that stretches nine miles inland. If you have binoculars, bring them to watch the swarms of carmine bee-eaters during the winter migrant season of November to April. At Kilifi is another centre for deep sea fishing and all the water sports. Cashew nuts are a major product of the area, with a large processing factory on the north side of the creek.

The Gedi mystery

Another 25 miles brings you to the mysterious ruined Arab city of Gedi, just north of Mida Creek. From the 13th century it flourished as a 25-acre walled settlement. But curiously its forest location went unrecorded in historic writings, even when the Portuguese were only ten miles away in Malindi.

Archaeologists reckon that Gedi was suddenly abandoned during the 18th century, leaving the forest to absorb the poorer dwellings of mud and thatch. But a stone Palace, neighbouring houses, a Great Mosque (one of seven that served the community) and a 14th-century pillar tomb are evidence of a prosperous Swahili lifestyle.

KENYA COAST

Watamu

A few miles away on the coast is the tranquil holiday resort of Watamu. The offshore Marine National Park offers breathtaking views by scuba, snorkel or glass bottom boat of the brilliant tropical fish that congregate at the coral gardens. Fish feeding is frowned upon by environmental purists, but it encourages shoals of fish to welcome the arrival of every boat.

Malindi

Eighty miles north of Mombasa, Malindi is a popular holiday resort with a blend of hotels and a local fishing village offering markets and shops in Arab African style. Serving an international clientele, many of the hotel staff also speak German and Italian.

A highlight is to visit the coral gardens of the Malindi Marine Park, which adjoins the northern end of the Watamu National Park. Both these reserves were created in 1968, to stop the plundering of coral and shells for the souvenir trade.

Malindi, as a long-standing rival of Mombasa, prospered under the Portuguese flag until power switched to Mombasa. But Malindi still flourished for the next 300 years from fishing and the slave trade, with weekly slave auctions by the Juma Mosque. The ban on slavery in 1873 wrecked the local economy, which did not revive until holidaymakers arrived in the 1930's.

Beach hotels began to mushroom, and the game-fishing fame of Malindi was sparked by personalities like Ernest Hemingway who held court in the bar of the Blue Marlin Hotel. In recent decades, Malindi has been the focus of major game-fishing tournaments.

Lamu Island

Some 80 miles north of Malindi along a dirt road, Lamu is unchanged from distant centuries. No cars are permitted on the island, thus preserving the atmosphere of 600 years ago. Historically the island came under the cultural influence of the 9th-century Persians, followed by a succession of Arabs, Indian merchants and Portuguese.

As a trading centre formerly based on ivory, spices, silks, perfumes and slaves, the island is like a miniature Zanzibar: a maze of Arab-style houses, centuries old, with heavily studded wooden doors, overhanging balconies and flower-filled courtyards.

7.5 Game fishing

Kenya offers some of the world's finest deep sea fishing, with great variety of species found close to shore. A day spent fishing is an adventure in itself.

The main billfish (sailfish and marlin) season runs from late November to mid or late March. But sailfish often come inshore during August as well. August to October is the tuna season. Most fish are passing through and not resident in the area. Although the professionals have a rough idea of what fish will be around – and when – the fish don't read the charts and don't pop up according to any kind of fixed schedule. So it's possible to catch fish throughout the year.

Game fishing is not just for seasoned anglers. Boat crews are well versed at introducing total newcomers to the sport and enjoy showing how it all works. Let the skipper know how much fishing experience you have and how much you want to be involved in the baiting and striking of fish.

The crew will happily prepare and put on ice any fish you catch and want to eat back at the hotel. Tipping of the crew is accepted with thanks but is by no means obligatory.

7.6 Try scuba diving

One of the glories of the Kenya coast is the long line of coral reefs which help keep out unwanted algae, barracudas and sharks, to ensure ideal conditions for water sports. The gorgeous colouring and marine life give added enchantment to everyone who comes viewing by snorkel, glass bottom boat, Arab dhow or scuba. Wherever you are staying, exploration of the reef or the spectacular Marine National Reserves of Watamu, Malindi or Kisite is easily arranged.

Qualified scuba divers rate the Kenya coast among the world's top three locations, along with the Red Sea and Australia's Barrier Reef. Many sub-aqua enthusiasts come specially for the diving, and arrive ready equipped with their diving certificate and logbook.

Dive schools are attached to most hotels, and many offer a complimentary lesson in the hotel pool. If you get a liking for the sport, it's possible to book a full course leading to a PADI certificate. Try it!

Chapter Eight

Kenya beyond the beaches

8.1 Geography

Kenya covers an area of 225,000 sq miles, stretching from 5 degrees north to 5 degrees south of the equator. Almost sitting on the equator is the centrally-located 17,057-ft Mount Kenya, from which the country takes its name.

Mount Kenya is Africa's second-highest mountain, topped only by 19,340-ft Kilimanjaro just across the border in Tanzania. Mountains dominate the geography of East Africa. A lowland coastal belt is only two to ten miles wide in the south, though north of Malindi and the Tana River the belt widens to a hundred miles.

From the coastal plain fringed by the coral reefs of the Indian Ocean, there is a sharp rise to an eastern plateau which then gradually climbs westwards to the 5,000-ft altitude of the Yatta Plateau.

The Kenya Highlands are bisected from north to south by the Great Rift Valley – the great geographical fault line which carves across the earth's surface from Lake Baikal in Russia, via Lebanon and the Red Sea, through Kenya and Tanzania to Mozambique.

Its most spectacular sector is through Kenya, where the Rift floor is between 30 and 40 miles wide and from 2,000 to 3,000 feet lower than the surrounding countryside. Lakes and extinct volcanoes mark the line of the Rift. From Lake Turkana in the north, the Rift includes Lakes Baringo, Bogoria, Nakuru and Naivasha, continuing to Lake Manyara in Tanzania. All these areas feature magnificent birdlife.

Within Kenya's borders there are great variations in terrain: from a tropical coastline to glacial ice, arid deserts, mountain massifs, rich savannahs, large lakes and dense forests.

The arid northeast and northwest and a large area of the southeast are virtually uninhabited, except for small nomadic populations. But the southwest and the central Kenya Highlands are much more fertile and comprise one of the most successful regions of agricultural production in Africa. This region carries some 85% of Kenya's total population.

On the western borders, Lake Victoria comes partly within Kenya's territory, and is the world's second largest freshwater lake. A combination of evaporation and cold air from the mountains helps create a local climate of regular daily rainfall in the Kericho area – perfect conditions for Kenya's tea industry.

8.2 History

Without entering into scientific arguments, it's generally accepted that the Great Rift Valley in Kenya and northern Tanzania was one of the earliest homes of man's ancestors – give or take a million years, depending on where one fixes the ancestral line.

Discoveries made by the Leakey family in Tanzania's Olduvai Gorge and beside Kenya's Lake Turkana are at the heart of the dating controversies.

Closer in time-scale, hunter-gatherers have been living in the area for the past 100,000 years. In the early centuries of the Christian era, Bantu tribesmen arrived and began planting crops and using metal tools.

From the 7th century AD, Arab and Persian traders came regularly to the coast, and established trading posts at Mombasa and other coastal locations. Their intermingling with Bantu peoples led to growth of the Swahili language and culture – an Islamic mixture of basic Arabic and Bantu and the later addition of Portuguese, Indian and English words.

European influence came with the Portuguese explorer, Vasco da Gama, who landed at Malindi in 1498 – having first been given an unfriendly welcome by Arab merchants at Mombasa.

Portugal v. the Arabs

Soon the coast and its trade routes were contested by the Portuguese, who captured Mombasa and built Fort Jesus. A struggle swayed back and forth, but control was completely regained by the Arabs in 1698, when a three-year siege of Fort Jesus ended in the recapture of

KENYA BACKGROUND

Mombasa by the Sultan of Muscat and Oman. Ruling from Zanzibar, the Arabs built a flourishing trade in ivory and slaves, sending caravans into the interior.

For Europeans, the interior remained an unmapped mystery until the mid-19th century. From 1850 numerous explorers and missionaries, including David Livingstone, set forth from the coast with various objectives: to find the source of the Nile, to convert the inhabitants and to end the slave trade.

Carving up Africa

In the general 'scramble for Africa', Germany and Britain agreed to divide East Africa into zones of influence – German East Africa from 1885 for Tanzania; British East Africa for coastal Kenya on a leasing agreement in 1887 from the Sultan of Zanzibar.

With that foothold, the British government established the East Africa Protectorate in 1895.

To develop the country, the next stage came from 1896 onwards, when work started on building a railway to link Mombasa with Uganda. Construction was rapid. To encourage immigration, the Kenya Highlands – traditional homeland of the Kikuyu people – were reserved for white-only settlement.

Elsewhere, Maasai herdsmen on prime grazing land were induced to move to other districts. Mainly the white settlers came from upper-crust England or in larger numbers from South Africa.

During the First World War, German forces invaded from Tanganyika and tried to cut the Mombasa-Nairobi railway line. But the South African General Jan Smuts in command of the Allied troops pushed them back, and Tanganyika became part of British East Africa.

Meanwhile, and in the following years, the Kikuyu people became increasingly restive. Some African chiefs and village headmen carried out lower-level administration. But a better-educated African elite agitated for political rights, and restitution of their lands. Finally open revolt erupted in the 1950's with the Mau Mau anti-settler terrorist campaign.

Majority rule was eventually agreed at a Lancaster House Conference in 1960. Jomo Kenyatta, having spent some years in prison, became President when Kenya gained independence in 1963. He remained President until his death in 1978, when he was succeeded by President Daniel arap Moi.

8.3 The economy

Kenya's most serious economic problem is an annual population growth rate of 3.6% - one of the highest in the world. In the meantime, Gross Domestic Product has kept only slightly ahead of population. Variable climatic conditions and acute pressure on arable land restrict much further growth in agriculture, the leading economic sector. Tea and coffee account for almost half the country's total export earnings.

Many of the unemployed flock in from the countryside to the principal cities, especially Nairobi, where they try to earn a living on the fringe. The problems are obvious to any visitor who drives through some of the capital's shanty suburbs.

Local industries

Manufacture is principally in the area of import substitution and small-scale production of consumer goods – plastics, furniture, textiles, soap, cigarettes, flour.

Tourism is one of the few areas of potential expansion, though there is a limit on how many visitors can tour the Game Reserves without damaging the habitat. The answer is to encourage more visits to lesser-known Parks, spreading the environmental impact. Meanwhile Kenya continues to run a major trade deficit.

8.4 Conservation

From the 1970's poaching became an extremely serious problem, when Somali gangs heavily armed with automatic weapons threatened the elephant and rhino populations with extinction. The lure was extremely high world prices for ivory and rhino horns.

By the late 1980's, an international outcry against the slaughter forced the Kenyan government to take much more decisive action against the poachers. At risk also was Kenya's future in the safari business.

In a dramatic gesture, President Moi personally set fire to large stocks of confiscated tusks, horns and animal skins. Poaching in Kenya has been drastically reduced by arming game rangers with modern weapons and authorising them to shoot poachers on sight. There is hope that the depleted elephant and rhino populations will now have a chance to recover.

Chapter Nine

Cash crops and fruit

For garden-lovers there's great pleasure in touring through the Kenyan countryside, and seeing first-hand how the tropical crops, fruits and vegetables are grown. There is great diversity, owing to variations in climate between lowlands and highlands, and zones of heavy rainfall in the mountains to arid conditions in the northeast towards Ethiopia and Somalia.

If you see large areas of chrysanthemums, they are grown for production of pyrethrum insecticide from the dried flowers. In the Lake Naivasha area are huge fields of flowers such as carnations, produced for the world market.

Plantation crops include sugar cane, coffee, tea, pineapples, citrus, rice, sisal, coconuts, peanuts and bananas. Smallholdings and backyard plots grow maize, beans, onions, sweet potatoes and other tubers for domestic consumption and local market sale. Patches of land also produce export crops such as winter vegetables and exotic fruits. You can see avocado trees, mangoes, papayas, passion fruit and cashew nuts.

Coffee
Kenyans take pride in their locally-grown but expensive Arabica coffee, which is cultivated mainly in the fertile Aberdare foothills due north of Nairobi. Kenyan coffee has a prime reputation on export markets, and yields a high proportion of Kenya's currency earnings, even though the total volume is tiny by international standards. The exceptional flavour, body and acidity helps improve the flavour of cheaper coffees with which it is blended. Kenyan coffee is also a key ingredient of a local liqueur called Kenya Gold.

The coffee tree is an evergreen some 12 feet high, with glistening dark green leaves. When harvested, the tiny berries yield about 1000 seeds to a pound.

Plants bear fruit after three years. White flowers are followed by green berries which turn red when ripe. The red skin is removed before drying. The bushes are pruned for ease of picking. Each bush can live over a hundred years, and may yield 20 kgs beans annually. As a labour-intensive crop, coffee provides a cash income to Kenya's quarter-million smallholders who each devote an acre or less to the shrubs. Larger plantations yield about a third of Kenya's total production.

Tea
During recent years, Kenya has matured as a major world supplier of tea, which is grown in areas which are less suitable for coffee. About one half of Kenya's production is grown by peasant farmers who tend an acre or two of the waist-high bushes.

The remainder comes from large plantations operated by major companies such as Brooke Bond. These big estates are especially located in the Kericho area of western Kenya, where the climatic conditions are ideal, permitting picking of the top leaves every two weeks. Quality standards are high and consistent, with export grades fetching top prices at the London auctions.

Bananas
A banana plantation provides year-round fruit. Bananas grow well in the lushly fertile coastal areas, and are also a backyard crop for domestic consumption and local sale. A close relative is the plantain, looking like a large green banana, and cooked as a vegetable.

Banana trees are planted 8 to 9 feet apart, and rapidly grow with fibrous stems that comprise 90% water, held in cells. The plant is hermaphrodite: male and female flowers on the same stalk. Reproduction takes place without pollination. The first flowers appear when the plant is about one year old.

Bananas are the female part of the flower, and at the tip of the flower stalk is the male organ. Each row of bananas is separated by large purple bracts, or petals, which are cut off to expose the bananas to the sun.

The bananas gradually turn upwards, and fatten. Harvesters give three rhythmic sweeps of a panga, with movements graceful as a ballet: one chop to bring the branch down within hand's reach, another to sever the stem, a third to chop off the branch completely. After removal of the fruit, the stems are used as fodder. The original plant dies, but is replaced by suckers.

CASH CROPS

Coconuts

Thousands of coconut palms flourish in coastal areas – slender and graceful trees which enhance the tropical-paradise image of Kenya's holiday beaches. As a commercial crop, the tree is cultivated mainly for oil extracted from the sun-dried copra. Crude oil is an ingredient in soap and cosmetics, while refined oil is used for cooking, and for manufacture of margarine and salad oils. The cake which remains after oil extraction is used for cattle feed.

Wayside vendors offer fresh coconut milk, scalping the fruit with a panga. People who stop for a drink also own the flesh of the coconut. But usually they don't bother, just leaving it with the street vendor. Coconut milk can double as a suntan lotion.

By-products help rank the coconut palm among the world's most useful trees. The outer casing makes good fertilizer, while the very strong coir fibre is used for rope-making, coarse brushes and matting. The second shell burns well as fuel. Palm leaves make an economy thatch.

Coconuts are disseminated by independent sea travel. The fibrous husk keeps the fruit afloat, while the tough skin prevents water-logging. Swept by tides and currents onto a distant shore, the nut germinates rapidly, even after four months' afloat.

Growing 100 feet tall, coconut palms begin to yield after six years, and remain productive for a century. If a fruit is harvested green from four months onwards, it contains mostly sweet milk. Otherwise the fruit takes a year to ripen, when the milk has become solid and oily to produce the coconut meat. An average tree bears over 40 nuts annually, yielding about 20 lbs of copra from which a gallon of oil can be extracted.

Sisal

One of Kenya's more important plantation crops is sisal, which looks like an enormous pineapple that sprouts long fibrous leaves reaching over six feet high. The sisal plant was introduced from Central America in 1892. The hard fibre is crushed and scraped, dried, combed and baled for export, or twisted into binder twine, ropes and cordage. Sisal is also used in other products such as matting, sacks and plaster boards, and even for upholstery purposes. But artificial fibres are taking over in many of these functions.

Chapter Ten

Shopping

Among the items to consider buying are wood carvings, copperware, East African precious and semi-precious gemstones and jewellery, hand printed cotton materials of traditional African design, brightly coloured Kangas, basketwork, ashtrays, local pottery, toys, soapstone carvings and paperweights, and of course Kenya coffee and a big pineapple.

The City Market in Nairobi and the Spice Market in Mombasa (behind the vegetable market) are especially interesting and can supply good gifts. In the Asian-run stores, oriental carpets and gold embroidered silk saris from India attract keen buyers.

Kenyans have great skill in wood carving. Their work, both decorative and useful, makes attractive souvenirs. Good examples can be bought quite cheaply from street vendors, curio shops or the wood-carving cooperative in Mombasa. Bookends, paper knives and salad servers are among the utility carvings. But the best craftsmen show their skill in beautifully carved animal and human heads. Ceremonial drums, beadwork and hunting spears make attractive ornaments.

Bartering is common at market stalls and at souvenir shops. You will know you have bid too low when the locals let you go away without a purchase!

Beach vendors sell various souvenirs and local crafts. They can be over persistent. Just be firm but friendly if you are not interested.

In Mombasa and Nairobi airports there are new, well-stocked duty free shops although it is advisable to check out the town prices first. Many prices are higher at the airports than in local shops.

Kenyans are currently doing their utmost to protect wildlife, and work closely with the World Wildlife Fund. It is illegal to buy and attempt to export ivory, animal skins, stuffed animals or coral.

Chapter Eleven
Eating and drinking

What is the food like? Generally it is British in style, especially in the game lodges. On safari, breakfast will be served at the most convenient time for all concerned. If you are taking a short dawn game drive then there'll be a wake-up cup of tea or coffee, with breakfast served on your return. Otherwise breakfast will be taken at the normal time, before starting the day's drive.

Breakfasts are generous: choice of cereal, porridge or cornflakes; fruit juice – orange, pineapple or grapefruit; pineapple slices or paw paw (papaya, with a twist of lemon juice); eggs cooked varied ways, bacon and sausage, with toast, marmalade, tea or coffee.

Lunch is often served buffet style: a soup; choice of cold cuts, salads and sometimes a hot choice; then cold sweets and gateaux, fruit, cheese and biscuits. Afternoon tea is served in many of the hotels.

Evening meals can feature a sea food cocktail, soup, a standard meat course of chicken, pork or beef, with the usual vegetables and desserts. In some hotels tea or coffee is included with main meals. There are ample opportunities to try the range of local fruits.

In the main centres, food has more of an international flavour, with Italian, French, Indian and Oriental restaurants, whilst the coast is renowned for a wide choice of seafood. There are some very good restaurants in Nairobi and Mombasa. Ask your tour rep for recommendations.

Seafood in local style can be quite delicious: a ground-base of rice, with cooked plantains or bananas, mussel and other shell-fish, fried shrimps, green peppers and varied mystery ingredients. Most visitors enjoy the many foods prepared in coconut milk.

When the opportunity arises, try the lobster dishes, or king crab, oysters or smoked tuna. On safari, mountain trout or lake perch are often on the menu.

All the drinks

All hotels and game lodges supply clean cold water in vacuum flasks by your bedside. See chapter 2, health section, for comments on tap water.

Pineapple juice is a favourite thirst-quencher; or passion fruit juice. You should certainly try coconut milk, served in its shell with a straw through the top. It can be enlivened with a slug of rum.

Alcohol

The local beer, a lager type, is good and reasonably priced. Tusker, Pilsner and White Cap are the familiar labels. Wines and spirits are usually imported and can be expensive. However, Kenya does produce its own white wine, in the Naivasha region, and it's well worth trying. An innovation of the past decade is papaya wine, white or rosé.

You'll also find that Kenya Ivory (similar to Baileys Irish Cream) makes an excellent after-dinner liqueur. Kenya Gold, coffee-flavoured like Tia Maria, is less expensive than other spirits, and some people like it.

In the safari lodges, drinks are usually more expensive than in town bars and hotels.

Chapter Twelve

Travel hints

12.1 Tipping

Hotel and restaurant bills usually include a 10-15% service charge. For exceptional service, friendly and attentive, something extra would be appropriate – as at any other upmarket location, but at your discretion. If service is not included, restaurant and bar waiters are accustomed to clients' leaving a 10% tip. A small tip is usual for porters, whilst 10% is normal for cabbies.

Depending on the circumstances, tipping always helps to smooth the way. Do not hesitate to ask local advice if in doubt. Do not tip in English money.

On safari a collection is normally made for the driver at the end of the tour. The usual gratuity is the equivalent of £1.50 per person per day.

Incidentally, the basic schooling of some village children is hampered by their lack of ballpoint pens and pencils. If you wish to bring some, your driver will advise how to ensure they reach the children.

12.2 Electricity

The electric current is 220 volts AC (3 pin), compatible with the UK, and normally with 2-pin round or 3-pin square plugs. Not all of the safari lodges have power sockets in the rooms. If you need to recharge batteries and your room has no socket, the reception staff can probably handle it for you.

Some hotels also provide sockets and power supply for 110-volt appliances with a flat 2-pin plug. But visitors from North America should still check whether their appliances have a dual voltage switch, though hotels can often lend a suitable transformer. Otherwise, bring a plug adaptor and a step-down transformer.

12.3 Kenyan time

Kenya is 3 hours ahead of GMT (+ 2 hours during British Summer Time); or 8 hours ahead of Eastern Standard Time (+ 7 hours during Summer Time). Kenya doesn't alter clocks for summer.

12.4 Phoning home

Making an international phone call can involve a wait. If there is a phone in your room then you can either dial direct or the hotel operator will make the connection. If the hotel has no phone lines in the rooms, calls can be made from reception.

It is sometimes difficult to get an international line, so don't expect an instant connection. The code for the UK is 000 44 followed by the area code (STD) and then the number. The zero should always be omitted from the STD code.

For example if you are phoning a friend in London, dial 000 44 171 followed by the local seven-digit number.

The code for North America is 000 1, followed by area code etc.

It's not easy to telephone whilst on safari as many of the lodges have a rather primitive telephone system, and mostly operate with radio phones. It can be very difficult to obtain an international line.

Beware of the cost involved! As a rough guide you should expect to pay £15 for any part of 3 minutes plus £5 for each further minute. Check the price first! Tariffs drop between 10 p.m. and 10 a.m.

The country code for Kenya is 254. From Britain dial 00 254 plus area code and number. Nairobi's area code is 2; Mombasa's 11.

12.5 Newspapers, radio and TV

Kenya has three English-language newspapers – *Nation*, *Kenya Times* and the *Standard*. They can be useful for information about local events, but may be rather limited in coverage of what's happening in Europe or North America.

London newspapers arrive a day or two after publication, with the price heavily loaded by the cost of air travel. For US news, the European editions of *The Wall Street Journal* and *International Herald Tribune* are available.

Likewise the standard international magazines such as *Newsweek* and *Time* are on sale in their regional editions.

Television

Hotel TV's give you the local Kenya television in English and Swahili, with wider choice offered by hotels that have satellite dishes. But the visitor can still feel cut off from home-flavoured news.

It's worth travelling with a short-wave radio, to pick up the regular on-the-hour news bulletins of the BBC World Service and Voice of America.

12.6 Security

Just like anywhere else in the world, it's prudent to take simple precautions against theft. Kenya does not have an excessive crime rate. But some crime is inevitable, especially in a country where your holiday spending money could equal a year's average wage.

In hotels, occasional break-ins can happen, and there is a pickpocket and bag-snatch risk especially in Nairobi. It's good standard policy to put your credit cards, traveller cheques, jewellery, passport and return ticket into a safe deposit box. The majority of hotels have a room safe at a small charge.

Outdoors, take particular care of handbags and wallets in crowded areas such as markets. Don't leave items of value on open view in a car. Don't wear expensive jewellery in built-up areas or on the beach. A small number of visitors to Kenya encounter harassment in areas outside the hotel grounds or off the hotel beach, and it is wise not to venture alone at night.

In the evening, ensure that a handbag has nothing of value in it. Late at night it's preferable to use a taxi and avoid carrying large wads of money. Don't go on romantic after-dark strolls along lonesome beaches and avoid parts of downtown Nairobi.

Reporting a loss

If you have the misfortune to experience any sort of crime, report it to your hotel, who will contact the police as necessary.

An official loss report is needed to make an insurance claim. It's always a sensible precaution to keep a separate note of travellers cheque and credit card numbers, together with the hot-line telephone numbers to ring in case of loss.

Incidentally, there's no need to take valuables, ticket or passport on safari. Typically, some hotels in Nairobi have safety deposit facilities available free, or for a small charge. Clients are advised to leave excess valuables and passport while on safari and collect them at the end of the circuit.

Your passport number can be entered on your Personal Details Card as this is all you need for overnight registration. Credit cards are accepted at most lodges. However, if you do need to take any valuables on safari there are safety deposit boxes in the lodges.

12.7 Photo hints

Film prices in Kenya are much higher than in Britain or USA. Reckon £5 for a 24-exposure roll of standard colour-print stock. Dependent on how keen a photographer you are, decide how many films you think you will need and then add plenty more! If you use a specialised film, it's even more essential to take an oversupply. Off-beat films are hard to find. For beach and town photography, slowish films around ASA 100 will give good results for colour prints.

For cameras that use batteries, replace them before travelling on holiday – and pack a spare set. Take flash for pictures of evening activities and entertainments.

Concentrate your picture-making on early morning or late afternoon. Noontime sun makes people squint, and the strong light on beaches casts very harsh shadows. Also, the midday sun gives too much glare, though a lens hood and a polarization filter can help overcome the problem.

Towards evening, dusk is of short duration. Capture that sunset picture quickly, before it disappears! Make your beach photos more interesting with a foreground palm tree as a frame or silhouette.

Lens protection

Game-reserve dust or fine sand on the lens can spoil results. Whenever the camera is not in use, keep the lens cap in place. Along dirt roads, keep equipment in a dust-proof bag until it's time for action. Bring some lens-cleaning tissue and a dust brush. Leave a skylight filter permanently in place – much cheaper to renew if vigorous cleaning causes scratches. Don't leave your camera lying in the sun, as heat can harm the film.

In the principal tourist locations, local people are accustomed to visiting shutterbugs with their desire to point cameras in every direction. Elsewhere, folk may be less tolerant of any invasion of their privacy.

Always ask the permission of tribesmen whom you meet on safari before taking their pictures. Permission will probably be given quite cheerfully, especially if a few coins change hands.

However, if you don't make a big production of it, you can still get colourful shots of people in characteristic activity. Position yourself by a monument or in a crowded market, or at a crossroads. With a wide-angle lens for close-up, or long-focus lens for more distant shots, you can discreetly get many of your local-colour pictures without irritating anyone.

Incidentally, it is forbidden to photograph the President, the Police, the Armed Forces or military installations.

Wildlife pictures

On safari, most visitors want a photographic record of their trip. Even though game-viewing vehicles get remarkably close to the animals, it's essential to go equipped with telephoto lenses. Many of the safari drivers are well accustomed to their clients' photo techniques, and often can manoeuvre the vehicle into a good position for pictures.

It's worth carrying a selection of different speed films, as the light can vary and is often not as bright as you might expect. A 200-mm or 300-mm telephoto lens is strongly recommended, though a standard lens can still be useful for close-ups of half-tame animals around safari lodges. The professionals use lenses of 600 mm or more, but these require tripods and are impractical for use in the average safari mini-bus.

Holding the camera steady is a big problem, as camera shake is magnified when using a telephoto. Resting your camera on a bean-bag helps to diminish the problem of engine vibration. But the chance of avoiding camera shake can be improved if the vehicle's engine is switched off, and if the other passengers can be persuaded not to jig around.

12.8 Learn some Swahili

Swahili is the national language of Kenya, but English is the commercial language, understood and spoken by most people in towns and cities. Each tribe has its own language. Children at school are taught English, Swahili and their tribal language.

The Swahili language is derived from a mingling of Bantu with Arabic and Persian. It's the lingua franca throughout Kenya and Tanzania, and also further afield. In written form it uses the Latin alphabet and is completely phonetic.

As in all destinations, a few local words can often give much additional pleasure. If you want to go deeper, it's not a difficult language to learn. Virtually every syllable ends with a vowel, with accent on the penultimate syllable. Thus, hello – jambo – is pronounced **ja**-mbo.

How are you?	Habari?
Very well	Mzuri sana
Please	Tafadhali
Thank you (very much)	Asante (sana)
Sorry!	Pole
Goodbye	Kwaheri
Yes	Ndiyo
No	Hapana
Good	Mzuri
How much?	Pesa ngapi?

12.9 Background reading

Field Guide to the Larger Animals of Africa – Jean Dorst, Collins
Field Guide to the Birds of East Africa – John Williams, Collins
Field Guide to the National Parks of East Africa – John Williams, Collins
Flame Trees of Thika – Elspeth Huxley, Penguin
People of Kenya – Joy Adamson, Collins & Harvill Press.

Chapter Thirteen
Further reference

13.1 Quick facts

Total land area: 220,000 sq miles.

Comparative area: 2.5 times the size of Britain; 5/6ths the size of Texas.

Indian Ocean coastline: 330 miles.

Land boundaries: 2,160 miles total; Ethiopia 535m, Somalia 424m, Sudan 144m, Tanzania 478m, Uganda 580m.

Land use: arable land 3%; meadows and pastures 7%; permanent crops 1%; forest and woodland 4%; other 85%.

Population: estimated 28 million, growth rate 3.6%.

Birth rate: 45 births/1,000 population.

Life expectancy at birth: 60 years male, 64 years female.

Total fertility rate: 6.4 children born per woman.

Ethnic divisions: Kikuyu 21%, Luhya 14%, Luo 13%, Kalenjin 11%, Kamba 11%, Kisii 6%, Meru 6%; Arab, Asian and European 1%.

Language: English and Swahili (official), and numerous indigenous languages.

Religion: Protestant 38%, Roman Catholic 28%, indigenous beliefs 26%, Muslim 6%.

Literacy: 69% (male 80%, female 58%).

Labour force: 9.2 million (includes unemployed). The total employed is 1.37 million, of which services account for 54.8%, industry 26.2% and agriculture 19.0%.

Capital: Nairobi, population over 2 million.

Administrative divisions: 7 provinces and 1 area; Central, Coast, Eastern, Nairobi Area, North-Eastern, Nyanza, Rift Valley, Western.

Independence: 12 December 1963 (from UK; formerly British East Africa).

Legal system: based on English common law, tribal law, and Islamic law; judicial review in High Court; constitutional amendment in 1982 made the Republic of Kenya a de jure one-party state.

Executive branch: president, vice president, Cabinet.

Legislative branch: unicameral National Assembly (Bunge).

Judicial branch: Court of Appeal, High Court.

Political party: Kenya African National Union (KANU).

Suffrage: universal at age 18.

Fiscal year: 1 July-30 June.

Military service: no conscription.

13.2 Public holidays and events

Kenya's basic annual public holidays are:
Jan 1 – New Year's Day
Good Friday
Easter Monday
May 1 – Labour Day
June 1 – Madaraka Day
Oct 10 – Moi Day
Oct 20 – Kenyatta Day
Dec 12 – Jamhuri Independence Day
Dec 25/26 – Christmas and Boxing Day

The Moslem community also celebrates 'Idd-ul Fitr' to mark the end of the Ramadan month of fasting. In 1997 that moveable feast came on February 8. Each subsequent year the date moves forward by 10 or 11 days, depending on the state of the moon.

The big national event is the famous Easter **Safari Rally**, which is claimed to be the toughest in the world. The course features some of the worst roads in Kenya, often made even stickier by heavy rains.

The **Kenya 2000** motor rally is held in May.

Popular local events are the agricultural shows organised by the **Agricultural Society of Kenya (ASK)**. Around a dozen are featured in different areas during the period of May to November. These lively gatherings are certainly worth a special journey.

13.3 Useful addresses

In UK:

Kenya Tourist Office, 25 Brook's Mews (off Davis St), London W1Y 1LF. Tel: (0171) 355 3144. Opening hours: 9-13 hrs and 14-17 hrs, Mon-Fri.

Kenya High Commission, 45 Portland Place, London W1N 3AG. Tel: (0171) 636 2371.

Kenya Airways, 16 Conduit St, London W1R 9TD. Tel: (0171) 409 0185.

In North America:

Kenya Tourist Office/Consulate, 424 Madison Avenue, New York, NY 10017. Tel: (212) 486 1300.

Kenya Tourist Office/Consulate, 9100 Wilshire Blvd, Doheny Plaza Suite 111-2, Beverly Hills, Los Angeles, CA 90121. Tel: (213) 274 6635.

Kenya Embassy, 2249 R St, NW, Washington DC 20008. Tel: (202) 387 6101.

Kenya High Commission, Gillia Building, Suite 600, 141 Laurier Ave, West Ottawa, Ontario K1P 5J3. Tel: (613) 563 1773-6.

In Kenya:

British High Commission, P.O. Box 30465, Upper Hill Road, Nairobi. Tel: (2) 714699. Fax: (2) 719082. Mombasa Consulate (11) 25913.

US Embassy, corner Moi Avenue and Haile Selassie Avenue, P.O. Box 30137, Nairobi. Tel: (2) 334141. Mombasa Consulate: (11) 315478.

Canadian High Commission, Comcraft House, Haile Selassie Ave, Nairobi. Tel: (2) 334033.

Australian High Commission, Development House, Moi Ave, Nairobi. Tel: (2) 334666.

Mombasa Tourist Office, Jubilee House (by the tusks), Moi Ave, P.O. Box 80091. Tel: (11) 223465.

Malindi Tourist Office, P.O. Box 421. Tel: (123) 20747.

Thomson's Agent in Kenya: United Touring Company, Fedha Towers, Moi Avenue, Muindi Mbingu Street, P.O. Box 42196, Nairobi. Tel: (2) 331960.

United Touring Company, Moi Avenue, P.O. Box 84782, Mombasa. Tel: (11) 316333.

Chapter Fourteen

Identify the wildlife

East Africa rates as one of the world's richest areas for sheer variety of wildlife, thanks especially to the range of different habitats.

Over eighty major animal species are resident in the wildlife sanctuaries of Kenya and northern Tanzania.

Although the Big Five get most of the publicity, Kenya is also a fabulous location for birdwatching. East Africa is home to over a thousand species of birdlife, from the vulture and the maribou stork to the tiny bee-eaters and sunbirds. A dedicated birdwatcher can often spot a hundred species in a day.

Likewise some 600 species of tropical butterflies are spread across the wide variety of vegetation and climatic zones. Equally there are myriads of moths, particularly during rainy weather.

For detailed, specialist coverage of all this choice of wildlife, bookshops offer good choice of heavyweight Field Guides – see recommended titles on page 71.

In this pocket guidebook, the following pages illustrate some of the animals and birds which a safari traveller is most likely to see, depending on the season when the journey is made.

Here are the principal groups:

Lion

Elephant

Buffalo

Leopard

Rhino

Cheetah

Giraffe

Lion – The only sociable big cat spends much of the day sleeping, licking, grooming and greeting family members by rubbing heads with one another. Lions hunt mainly at night or early morning, in groups. A pride consists of related females and their cubs; or a group of males who have a range which they patrol and defend. Within this range live one or more prides of lionesses whom the males join for mating purposes.

Elephant – The largest living land animals, they have a highly developed social order. A herd is most likely to be a family unit, or an all-male group. Daughters remain within the same herd with mothers, grandmothers etc, while males leave at adolescence. Females give birth at about 13 years, and the gestation period is 22 months. Elephants can live up to 60 years.

Buffalo – These massive animals of ox-like build are distributed in very large herds. Adults have sparse, usually black, coats and massive horns. They are fond of wallowing, so are usually found near water. Buffalo can be an even match against lions, fiercely defending their young, and can be dangerous to man.

Leopard – A usually solitary big cat. Markings are in roseate clusters, black on a tawny coat (unlike the cheetah's which are in single spots). Excellent climbers, they often drag their kill up into a tree. Their voice is a grunted cough, or like wood being sawn.

Rhino – The black rhino is a solitary animal, resting during the day and feeding mostly at night, dawn and dusk. The prehensile lip enables it to grasp leaves, twigs and young shoots. White rhinos are larger, with wide mouth and square lip adapted to grazing. Rhinos have good sense of hearing, but poor eyesight.

Cheetah – More lightly built than the leopard, its tawny coat is scattered with numerous small round black spots, and it has a long black 'tear' mark from the corner of the eye to the mouth. It is extremely fast in rapid sprint when hunting (up to 75 mph) but cannot sustain this speed. Cheetah is found in open and semi-arid areas.

Giraffe – There are three sub-species. The reticulated giraffe is deep chestnut brown with a dividing network of fawn lines. The Maasai giraffe has dark brown irregular patches on a fawn background. Rothschild giraffes have white-sock forelegs.

Gnu

Topi

Hartebeest

Sable
Antelope

Eland

Waterbuck

Zebra

Uganda
Kob

78

Gnu or **Wildebeest** – A large antelope with massive head and shoulders in contrast to the slender hind quarters. Curved horns, slatey-grey coat with dark streaks on back and sides; white beard, black mane and tufted tail. Gnus live in open plains, and make spectacular migrations. They are very vocal, snorting and grunting.

Topi – Long faced, medium-sized antelope with ridged horns and sloping back; reddish brown in colour, with dark markings on face, shoulders and upper legs. In the dry season topis form herds with hundreds of other antelopes and zebras.

Coke's Hartebeest – Of similar size to the wildebeest, but with a lighter body. Sandy colour all over with ridged upward-curving horns. Congregate in large herds on open grassland throughout southern Kenya.

Sable antelope – Stands almost 5 ft high with a very dark coat and long swept-back horns. Underparts, rump and face are white. Found in small herds in lightly wooded areas of the Shimba Hills.

Eland – Very large, almost cow-like antelope weighing up to a ton. Males grey, females reddish fawn with pale lateral stripes around body. Both males and females have powerful horns with a corkscrew twist, enabling them to break off twigs for feeding.

Waterbuck – Medium-sized heavily built antelope. The males have majestic horns, ridged and backward-curving. Lives near water, and will take to the water if pursued. The shaggy grey brown coat is water repellant, with a distinctive white crescent around the rump. Waterbuck emit a strong, musky odour which deters predators.

Uganda Kob – A medium-sized antelope with red-gold coat, white underparts and white area around eyes. Ridged horns curve slightly backwards. It needs to drink daily, so prefers to live near water. Kobs live in herds and the males fight savagely for their harems.

Zebra – There are two species. Burchell's zebra is more common with broad black stripes. Grevy's zebra has narrow stripes and a white belly. The stripe pattern of every zebra is slightly different. At dawn and dusk the stripes blend to greyness when the zebra would be at most danger from predators.

Grant's Gazelle

Thomson's Gazelle

Kudu

Gerenuk

Dik-Dik

Oryx

Impala

Klipspringer

80

Grant's Gazelle – Medium sized, fawn in colour with white underparts and hind quarters, backward curving lyre-shaped horns. Bucks actively defend their rights to harems of about a dozen females. In the dry season they migrate in big herds with other browsing animals.

Thomson's Gazelle – Smaller than Grant's gazelle with shorter backward curving horns. Fawn coat with white underparts and very distinctive black band across lower side of body and hind legs. It twitches its tail frequently. Large herds gather in the dry season with Grant's gazelles, zebras and gnus.

Lesser Kudu – Medium sized antelope with large rounded ears which give them acute hearing. Smaller and more graceful than the greater kudu, they are distinguished by about a dozen narrow white stripes running down the flanks. Males are brown grey and have spiral horns; females are a reddish fawn.

Gerenuk – Large 'giraffe-necked' gazelle with long slender legs and small head; reddish brown coat with white underparts. Males have thick ringed horns. Lives in bush country in pairs or small family parties, and often stands on its hind legs to feed. The gerenuk seldom needs to drink, getting enough moisture from its leafy diet.

Dik-dik – Smallest of the antelopes, they weigh about 9 lbs, and are very shy. Greyish brown in colour with long nose and large luminous eyes. Lives in pairs or family groups in dry bush country or at the foot of a kopje with thickets for shelter.

Beisa Oryx – Large antelope, reddish grey body with black stripe along spine and lower side; white underparts. The face is strikingly marked in black and white, and both sexes have long, narrow ridged horns. Lives in dry open bush, in pairs or small family parties.

Impala – Medium sized, graceful antelope. Coat reddish brown, dark on back, shading to light below. Males have very long slender horns, lyre-shaped. Lives in territorial groups in savannah or woodlands.

Klipspringer – Goat-sized, thick set, rough-coated antelope with olive brown, speckled grey coat. Stands on tips of narrow, almost cylindrical, hooves. Mates for life, and lives in pairs or small family groups in scrub and savannah country.

Serval

Large-spotted
Genet

Bat-eared
Fox

Mongoose

Hare

Wart Hog

Crocodile

Hippo

Gecko

82

Serval – Long-legged cat of medium size with yellowish brown coat, banded, striped and spotted with black; short tail, black tipped. Lives in the open savannah or bush, always near water.

Large-spotted Genet – Cat-like with narrow pointed face; short pale grey or buff coloured fur with black and reddish spots of varying sizes. Tail heavily ringed with dark brown. It is found in open scrub and woodland. Nocturnal, it takes to the trees for safety.

Bat-eared fox – Rather like a jackal but smaller, with very large ears; grey or buff coloured coat, black muzzle, white forehead, black lower limbs and black-tipped bushy tail. Found in open country.

Mongoose – Four varieties occur in Kenya. Dwarf mongoose is small with dark brown coat, inhabits burrows in small packs. White-tailed is large with very dark grey fur and long black legs; solitary. Slender mongoose is dark red brown, with long black-tipped tail; solitary. Banded mongoose is dark grey with narrow black bands around back from about the middle to the tail base; lives in packs of up to thirty.

Hare – A common small mammal found in bush and scrubland. Buff to greyish fur, with white underparts.

Wart Hog – Sparse bristly coat with long stiff hair on neck and shoulders. Wart-like growths on face which are bigger in males than in females; large curved tusks. Wart hogs are fond of wallowing in mud. Usually seen in family groups in open grassland.

Crocodile – Can be watched basking on sand banks by the riverside. Do not approach too close, as they have a surprising turn of speed! The Nile Crocodile grows to 20 ft or more, and has a voracious appetite.

Hippo – Ponderous with massive head and barrel-shaped body, hairless dark grey skin. Often seen in water with just head showing. With webbed feet, it is an excellent swimmer and diver – can submerge for six minutes or so, and walk on the bottom under water. Hippo are safe to watch from a river bank, but be wary if met on land!

Gecko – Small lizards which can run up walls and across ceilings, thanks to adhesive pads on their toes. They live on insects and are nocturnal.

Sykes
Monkey

Baboon

Patas
Monkey

Bush Baby

Hyrax

Vervet
Monkey

Jackal

Hyena

Wild Dog

MONKEYS & SMALL PREDATORS

Anubis Baboon – Large solidly-built monkey with olive brown fur and long tail. Male has thick mane, and long canine teeth and is bigger than the female. They live in groups of 30-100, throughout open areas.

Sykes Monkey – Long-tailed, with olive brown fur, darker across shoulders and lower limbs; white around the head. Lives amongst trees in family groups.

Patas Monkey – Large, with gingery red and white coat; dark marking around eyes. More at home on the ground, it is a sociable animal, living in small groups. The male is almost twice the size of the female.

Bush Baby (Galago) – Two of these very long-tailed species: the grey Senegal; and the thick-tailed Galago which is double the size, with pale grey fur tinged with brown. They both have large round eyes and large ears. Tree-dwelling and nocturnal, they live in small groups. Their crybaby wail carries over long distances.

Vervet Monkey – Slender, medium sized, with light olive-grey fur, black face and white cheek tufts; and white on underparts of limbs and chest. Family groups live near water at forest edges and savannahs.

Hyrax – Three species of these small animals: Bush Hyrax has grey fur; Rock Hyrax is larger, with brown fur; and the Yellow-Spotted. Despite their size and appearance they are distantly related to the elephant. They are sociable and good climbers.

Jackal – Three types of jackal: side striped, golden and black-backed. About the size of a fox, with longer legs. They eat wild fruits and seeds, small birds, mammals and carrion. Their bark is a familiar sound in the African night.

Spotted Hyena – Powerfully built animal, especially in forequarters; broad head with dark muzzle; light yellowish grey body with dark spots; crest of coarse hair down back. Hyenas live in groups, mostly feed on carrion, but also hunt in packs. Their noisy calls rise to a scream that could be described as laughter.

Wild dog – Skinny long-legged animal with yellowish coat blotched with white and black patches; large head and big round ears. Lives in organised packs of 10-20 in open country, and hunts animals up to large antelope in size.

Yellow-billed Oxpecker

S. African Hoopoe

Quail Finch

White-backed Vulture

Kori Bustard

Secretary Bird

Ground Hornbill

Maribou Stork

Ostrich

Yellow-billed Oxpecker – Brown head, back and wings, buff chest. Lives with larger animals, wild and domestic, eating the ticks from their backs.

South African Hoopoe – Plumage brown, chest buff, black and white on wings and tail, crested head. Feeds on ground insects, continually tapping earth with its slender, curved bill.

Quail finch – Small birds with greyish brown back, white chest, and throat barred black. Found in swampy areas and grassy plains, they gather in small flocks and make a distinctive metallic chirruping in flight.

White-backed Vulture – Brown plumage with distinct white back, short white down on head and neck, wings and tail tipped black. Gathers in large flocks around a kill, and is fearless of man. Seven species of vulture occur in Africa.

Kori Bustard – One of the 11 species of Bustard. A large bird, about 5 ft high. Top of head black with crest, long neck barred black and white, dark back, white underparts. These birds of open country are beneficial to agriculture as they eat vast quantities of locusts and other insects.

Secretary Bird – Grey plumage with black wing feathers, crested head, long tail and long legs. Stands some 3 ft high, and lives in open country, usually in pairs. Kills snakes with a powerful stamp of its foot, and is protected by law.

Ground Hornbill – Largest of the Hornbills, of which there are 20 species in Africa. Black plumage, face and neck red, and bare in front. Hornbills are distinguished by the casque which tops the beak in varying shapes and sizes. A turkey-like bird, which is found in open country. Its call is a deep grunting, lion-like in sound.

Marabou Stork – Dark grey-green back, white body, bare head, chest and neck. The Marabou is more like a vulture than a stork in habits, living mainly on carrion.

Ostrich – Largest of living birds – male about 7 ft in height, with black body, white wings. Found on plains or among open thorn bush, usually in small parties. They have superb eyesight, and are very fast runners.

Chestnut Banded
Sand Plover

White
Pelican

Cape
Wigeon

Darter

Black-winged
Stilt

Avocet

Yellow-billed
Stork

African
Spoonbill

Lesser
Flamingo

Pelican – There are two species: white- and pink-backed pelican. A large, well-known bird, it inhabits lakes as well as coastal bays and inlets. The distensible throat pouch below the bill serves as a dip-net whilst fishing.

Chestnut Banded Sand Plover – Pale grey and white, with light chestnut band across chest. Usually seen in pairs or small parties, along lake shores. A restless, noisy bird, 28 species occur in East Africa.

Cape Wigeon – Medium-sized, light coloured bird; head and back flecked with black. Plentiful on Rift Valley lakes, its pale colour and white head make it conspicuous in flight.

Black-winged Stilt – Black and white bird, with straight, slender black bill; long red legs and feet. Found in or near water. Trails legs in flight, and has a piping cry.

Darter – A cormorant-like bird. When out of water, it is often seen drying its outstretched wings. Darters have a very noticeable kink in the long neck. Dark plumage; head and neck dark chestnut, with white stripe down side.

Avocet – Black and white bird with long upward-curving beak. Usually seen in small flocks, wading and feeding in shallow lake water.

Yellow-billed Stork – Also known as a wood ibis. White, with black and crimson on wings and tail; bare red head and yellow bill. Mostly seen on sand banks, shallow lakes and along the coast. Its call has been likened to a squeaky hinge.

Spoonbill – White plumaged bird with blue-grey bill and pinkish feet. Seen in small parties, wading and feeding in shallow water. Its large flat bill – spoon shaped at the tip – is used to scoop weeds and molluscs from the mud.

Lesser Flamingo – There are two species of flamingo. The Lesser has wings blotched with crimson; bill red, tipped with black. The Greater Flamingo has white plumage, and wings tinged with crimson, only noticeable in flight; black tipped bill, very long legs. Both species are found in vast numbers on the larger lakes of the Rift Valley.

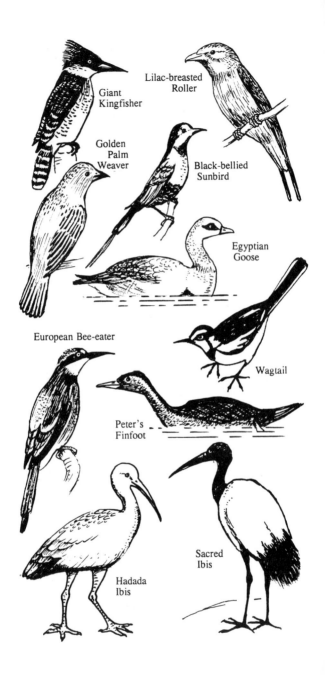

Giant Kingfisher

Lilac-breasted Roller

Golden Palm Weaver

Black-bellied Sunbird

Egyptian Goose

European Bee-eater

Wagtail

Peter's Finfoot

Hadada Ibis

Sacred Ibis

Giant Kingfisher – Largest of the kingfishers, lives close to water, and feeds mainly on fresh-water crabs and fish. Black crested head, streaked with white. Chest white in female, chestnut in male.

Lilac-breasted Roller – A noisy, colourful bird, showy in flight, with green head, brown back, lilac chest. Eight varieties are found in Kenya.

Golden Palm Weaver – About the size of a sparrow. Bright golden plumage in male, duller in female. Numerous varieties of weavers and waxbills live along rivers or near the coast; easily spotted by their colonies of elaborately woven hanging nests of grass and twigs.

Black-bellied Sunbird – A small bird with dark metallic plumage. Splash of orange on chest in male; olive-green brown in female. Feeds mainly on insects and tree flowers among the higher branches. Recognised by long tail feathers and slender down-curved beak. There are many species of sun birds.

Egyptian Goose – Chestnut back, white body, chestnut patch around eye. Feeds in evening on open plains, enjoying young grass. Roosts in trees.

European Bee-eater – Chestnut back and head, green chest and tail, long curved beak. Insect eaters, they are found in all types of country, usually amongst trees.

African Pied Wagtail – A riverside bird, recognised by its black and white plumage. Wagtails are found in nearly every village, and are regarded as good luck.

Peter's Finfoot – Dark green back, speckled white. White chest and belly. Its habitat is among the banks of densely wooded streams; swims low in the water.

Hadada Ibis – Brownish grey head, neck and underparts; bronze back and iridescent green wings; tail and wings tipped blue-black. Inhabits wooded streams and mangrove swamps. Its alarm call is easily recognised: "*ha, ha, ha-ha-ha*".

Sacred Ibis – Venerated in ancient Egypt, but no longer found there. A very distinctive bird, pure white with bare black head and neck. Wings dark tipped, tail plumes blue-black. Widely distributed in wetlands, it nests in flat-topped thorn trees in company with herons and egrets.

Sooty Gull

Mangrove Kingfisher

Crab Plover

Green Shank

Layard's Black-headed Weaver

Fischer's Turaco

Curlew

Long-tailed Cormorant

Black-headed Heron

Sooty Gull – Head and throat dark brown; green bill, dark back and wings, white belly; grey chest with white neck band. It's the commonest gull, often seen in harbours or sitting on rocks, and chasing terns to rob them of food. Ten species of gulls occur in East Africa.

Mangrove Kingfisher – Grey head, with white stripe by eye, red beak; back, tail and wings bright blue; pale grey chest. This bird is often seen drying its wings, perched by the side of a muddy creek or mangrove swamp.

Crab Plover – Black and white bird with heavy black beak, grey legs and feet. Small flocks feed along rocky shores. They are noisy birds, not shy of man.

Green Shank – Pale brown back and neck, streaked white and brown. Throat and underparts white; long legs are yellowish green. A large species of wader, this winter visitor is common both on fresh and salt waters.

Layard's Black-headed Weaver – Black head and bill, golden neck; back and wings mottled yellow and black; bright yellow below. It's a common and widespread weaver, nesting in noisy colonies. Weavers are a very large family, 163 species being recorded.

Fischer's Turaco – Back and tail greenish blue; head, neck and chest green; crimson on head crest, beak, back of neck and wings. A poor flier, it climbs and hops and glides from tree to tree.

Curlew – Plumage mottled buff and black, white underbody. Feeds in shallow water, and nests in flocks at the edge. Whimbrel is a similar but smaller bird, seen in the same habitat.

Long-tailed Cormorant – Small cormorant, velvety black except for some silvery grey on wings. Found in large flocks on lakes and coast. From a distance, flocks in flight look like ducks. The larger white-necked cormorant is found only on lakes.

Black-headed Heron – Grey plumage; back of neck and head with crest black; white throat. Found inland as well as on coast, but occasionally nests in towns. Fifteen species of heron have been recorded in East Africa.

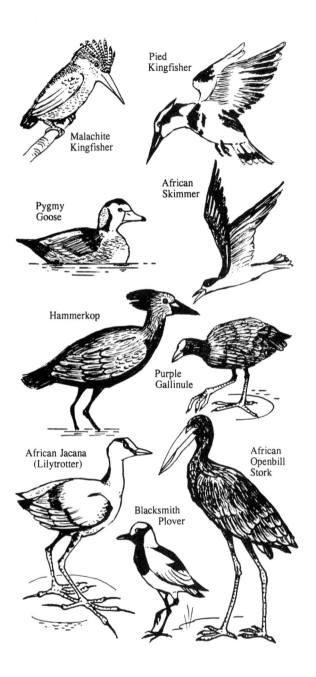

Malachite
Kingfisher

Pied
Kingfisher

African
Skimmer

Pygmy
Goose

Hammerkop

Purple
Gallinule

African Jacana
(Lilytrotter)

Blacksmith
Plover

African
Openbill
Stork

LAKE & SWAMP BIRDS

Malachite Kingfisher – Crested head, greenish blue and black; throat white, chest tawny, back bright blue. One of the most common kingfishers, very fast in flight. Watches for small fish and dragonflies from waterside perch.

Pied Kingfisher – Black back, streaked with white; black bands on wings, tail and chest. A common, noisy bird, its favourite perch is a tree stump. Its food, entirely fish, is located whilst hovering over water; and then plunging headlong.

Pygmy Goose – A small, beautiful bird, like a duck in size. Head black and green; face and neck white; back is a dark bottle green; body chestnut, white below; white bar on wing. It frequents bays and small lakes.

African Skimmer – Brownish black on head and back, otherwise white. A remarkable bird, obtaining its food by skimming the water surface with its unique bill. The lower mandible of its beak is somewhat longer than the upper, and flattened to form a scoop.

Hammerhead – Also known as **Hammerkop**, is so called because its crests, bill and neck form a hammer shape. Wholly brown plumage, with black bill and feet. Most remarkable is its enormous domed nest which can weigh around 150 kgs – some 3 cwt! Building takes many months, but the nest can then be used for years with constant additions. Frogs form its basic diet.

Purple Gallinule – Large blue bird with green back, red legs and feet. Lives in dense swamps and reed beds, feeding on seeds, insects and flower buds. Frequently seen on Lake Naivasha.

Lily-trotter – the **African Jacana** – Maroon brown with white neck; wing tips black; legs and feet red. The very long toes and claws enable it to walk over pools covered with water lilies.

African Openbill Stork – All-glossy black plumage. Heavy bill, open for part of its length. Mainly haunts fresh water, living on mussels and water snails. Often seen in large flocks.

Blacksmith Plover – Very visible in its black, white and grey plumage, the name comes from its loud and metallic "*tik-tik-tik*" call.

Wildlife Index